REBELLION
AT CHRISTIANA

REBELLION AT CHRISTIANA

by MARGARET HOPE BACON

Crown Publishers, Inc., New York

For their help in the preparation of *Rebellion at Christiana* I would like to thank Mrs. Bernard Levi Pownall and Hugh Douglass of Sadsbury Township; Eleanor Mayer and Jane Rittenhouse at the Friends Historical Library, Swarthmore; Edwin Bronner and Barbara Curtis at the Quaker Collection at Haverford. Thanks are also due to Beth Binford for typing, Ted Hetzel for photography, Sanderson Caesar for art work, and my husband Allen Bacon for his patience.

The author gratefully acknowledges *The Atlantic Monthly* for permission to use portions of William Parker's account of his life.

10 9 8 7 6 5 4 3 2

FOR PETER

CONTENTS

FOREWORD

ONE OF THE MOST EXCITING CHAPTERS IN THE HIStory of the United States is the story of the underground railroad. This was the name given to a system that grew up in the decades preceding the Civil War to help escaping slaves on their journey from the South to Canada and freedom. Most Americans have read vivid accounts of slaves hidden in root cellars, of dangerous trips in the dead of night, of hairbreadth escapes from slave catchers.

These stories have usually been based on accounts written by men and women who were alive at the time of the underground railroad, and who recalled the events in their old age. Naturally some of the details were fuzzy. Naturally, too, the authors gave most of the credit for the successful operation of the escape routes to their friends and neighbors who were white like themselves.

Today, when historians consult the records of the underground railroad that actually exist, they find that the black community played a much more important role in the operation of the escape routes than had previously been acknowledged. In a number of cities black people organized vigilance committees. The committees served as intelligence headquarters for the railroad, coordinating the escapes and warning communities in advance when slave catchers were on the way. It was fellow blacks who conducted daring rescues, freeing escaped slaves from marshals and even from jails, and setting them on their way north again.

Rebellion at Christiana is the story of the most dramatic of these rescues. William Parker, himself an escaped slave, had organized the blacks in lower Lancaster County, Pennsylvania, for mutual self-defense. When a slave owner from Maryland arrived at Christiana in the fall of 1851 with a posse to help him recapture four escaped slaves, Parker and his comrades fought to protect them. In the battle the slave owner was killed, and several of his party wounded. The four slaves escaped.

If that were all there was to it, Parker's rescue would be merely an exciting story. But the Christiana riot had another significance. In the course of trying to recapture the four slaves, the United States marshal had ordered two local white residents to aid him, as he was empowered to do by the Fugitive Slave Law. The two refused, being conscientiously opposed to maintaining the institution of slavery.

In the overheated imaginations of the frightened Marylanders, the two not only refused to come to their aid, but actually urged the blacks on to armed resistance. The men from Maryland jumped to the conclusion that the two Pennsylvania men had acted on the basis of a conspiracy to resist federal authority in the recapture of slaves.

The South in 1851 was on the verge of seceding from the Union if the Fugitive Slave Law was not enforced. In order to show the South that the law would be enforced and to keep the Union together, the federal government decided to try the Christiana rebels—white and black alike—for treason against the United States.

For a few weeks the Christiana treason trial brought into sharp focus all the great issues plaguing the United States ten years before the outbreak of the Civil War: the authority of the federal government to enforce the laws upholding slavery, a system that many of its citizens strongly opposed; the right of United States citizens to refuse to obey a law they did not believe in; the right of the South to conduct its own way of life without interference; and the morality of slavery itself.

In different forms these same issues are with us today, as men and women try to understand the revolutionary impulse, to use civil disobedience, and to deal with government when it no longer seems to reflect the wishes of the people.

The story of the Christiana riot is also important to us because we are lucky enough to have William Parker's own account of the event. Through it we can learn what the black perspective was over a hundred years ago on a series of events important to black history and important to the history of our nation as a whole.

CHAPTER 1

Trouble in Sadsbury Township

J UST WEST OF THE SMALL TOWN OF CHRISTIANA, IN
Sadsbury Township, Lancaster County, Pennsylvania, a wide valley opens out and runs for miles between two ridges of wooded hills. Intersected by a swift
stream, rich in flat fertile fields, Chester Valley today
is a picture of peace and serenity. But it has not always
been so.

One evening in the early 1840s two men driving a
covered wagon stopped at a small tenant house on the
north side of the valley and knocked on the door. When
a black woman answered they asked her where her husband might be found. They had heard, they said, of his
skill as a fence and rail maker, and they needed his
services for a job in the next county.

Not suspecting any trouble, the woman told them
that her husband had been working all day on a job up
the valley, and was probably on his way home. The two
men thanked her, and set off down Valley Road in the
direction she indicated.

Dusk was just beginning to settle along the length

of the great valley. The woman decided to stay outdoors and await her husband's return. For some reason the men's visit was beginning to make her anxious. She had just decided to start down the road to meet him when she heard from a distance her husband's voice screaming for help, then the rapid beat of horses' hooves.

The men who had asked after her husband must have been slave kidnappers! As quickly as she could the woman ran to the next farm and blurted out her short but terrible story. The farmer, a Quaker, immediately mounted his swiftest horse and went in pursuit, meanwhile sending word for other like-minded neighbors to join him. All that night the farmers scoured the valley and the roads leading south to Maryland. It was no use. The kidnapped man was never heard from again.

Slave kidnappings such as this were a common occurrence in Sadsbury Township throughout the 1840s. Many of the black men and women working on the farms in lower Lancaster County were actually escaped slaves who had slipped across the border from Maryland into Pennsylvania. Many other blacks were legally free, having been set at liberty by their Quaker masters many years ago. No matter; they were always in danger of being seized by unscrupulous slave agents and sent south to fit the description of some actual runaway slave.

The fence and rail maker had lived in Sadsbury for many years, and was thought to be free. In the case of his kidnapping, the neighbors suspected the Gap gang, a band of outlaws with headquarters on the north side of Mine Ridge, a range of hills stretching all the way from Gap, in the northwest corner of Sadsbury Township, to Lancaster.

Led by two men named William Baer and Perry Marsh, the Gap gang raided farms and stole horses from the peaceful Mennonite farmers who lived in Pequea Valley, north of Mine Ridge. But they also organized a system of informers who would alert them to the arrival of new blacks from the South, as well as new descriptions of runaway slaves. Baer was a party to so many successful kidnappings that the blacks were terrified whenever he showed up.

Serving the Gap gang as an informer was an itinerant clock mender, William Padgett. Padgett went from farm to farm, ostensibly to keep farm timepieces in good shape, but really to discover what new black men or women had been taken on as farmhands. An escaped slave himself, Padgett was so light-skinned that he could pass for white when it suited him. Besides wandering about the township with his clock-mending tools, Padgett worked as a hired hand at the Brown farm, between Gap and Christiana. People were suspicious of him, but for many years nothing was proved.

Shortly after the fence and rail maker was kidnapped, another black nicknamed "Tom-up-in-the-barn," who lived in a tenant house on the farm of Caleb Brinton, was on his way to thresh one summer morning when he was evidently picked up by kidnappers. No one ever knew whether he had been an escaped slave or not, and no one ever heard what happened to him. His abduction, too, was blamed on the Gap gang.

These kidnappings made the farmers of Sadsbury suspicious and truculent when southern slave owners armed with the law came looking for actual escaped slaves. The slave owners or their agents rarely bothered to obtain or show a warrant; the farmers were never sure when an escaped slave was being captured or a free black kidnapped. Many of them were deeply opposed to slavery anyway. They did not much care to cooperate in returning a black man or woman to slavery.

Ever since 1787, when the United States Constitution was ratified, a small but steady stream of slaves had escaped north, many through Lancaster County. At first there were only a few isolated cases, but by 1800 there began to be many more. For one thing, some of the northern states, including Pennsylvania, had enacted laws calling for the gradual emancipation of their own slaves. For another, the lot of the southern slave had become a great deal worse since the invention in 1793 of the cotton gin. This machine removed seeds from cotton mechanically and rapidly and made it profitable for planters to use huge gangs of slaves to cultivate increasingly large crops. At about the same time the mass cultivation of sugarcane became a major agricultural industry, also demanding massive slave labor.

In the cotton and cane-growing plantations the slave worked as a member of a gang, under the lash of an overseer whose job it was to harvest as large a crop as possible. As the need for slaves in the Deep South grew, a slave living in Virginia, Maryland, or Delaware became increasingly subject to being sold South. Families were broken up and children taken from their mothers. It was a brutal system, and it brutalized the masters as well. Some remained sensitive, but the majority were forced by the system to think of the slaves not as people, but as pieces of useful equipment. Some masters began to select young female slaves for their own sexual pleasures. Black husbands and wives were occasionally separated for this reason.

Although open, organized rebellion was so difficult that it occurred only two or three times, the majority of slaves developed techniques of passive resistance. They worked slowly and played dumb when it suited their purposes. A small minority managed to slip away. Hiding in swamps, guided by the north star, often chased by bloodhounds, many brave men and women made the perilous trip north.

Once a slave reached a northern state, he or she could usually count on the assistance of abolitionists, men and women opposed to slavery who hid the fugitives, gave them food and clothes, and transported them to some other family, either farther north or farther from detection. Sometimes they went to work for a local farmer who might need an extra hand. Here they might live for years without being found. In the decade immediately preceding the Civil War, however, it became necessary to get the slaves clear to Canada. Often it was free blacks in the North who organized the escapes and provided hiding places.

Pursuing southern slave owners were baffled by the way the slaves seemed to disappear once they got across the border. "There must be an underground railroad around here," one had said. The name stuck. From that time on the system of helping slaves go North was called the underground railroad, and there were stations, conductors, trunk lines, and branch lines all the way to Canada.

Unfortunately, not all the men and women in the border states were good Samaritans, and some took advantage of the presence of the escaped slaves and the free blacks. Slave owners who had lost their slaves offered generous rewards for recapture, sometimes as much as two hundred dollars, a fortune in those days. The descriptions of escaped slaves that they sent North were often quite vague: "Lost, black male, about thirty, answers to the name of Job. Stocky." Almost any black man or woman of about the right size or shape was in danger of fitting the description. There grew up a lucrative trade in slave kidnapping; snatching free blacks right off the farm where they were working, claiming they fit a particular description, and selling them South as fugitives.

Because of its location just north of the Mason-Dixon line, Lancaster County was embroiled from earliest times over the issue of slavery. Slaves escaping from Maryland owners constantly slipped across the border into the neighboring state and many settled down as farmhands for Pennsylvania farmers. When slave owners and their agents came North to hunt slaves, they generally looked first in the lower townships of Lancaster County. Slave kidnappers, too, frequented the area. There were many incidents of trouble between Marylanders and Pennsylvanians, inflaming the border rivalry that had been present since colonial times between the people of the two states.

The town of Columbia, on the Susquehanna River, became a natural escape route for slaves running away from Maryland, as well as from the deeper South. Philadelphia with its large population of abolitionists, both black and white, was only sixty-five miles away. From here one could take a boat or train farther north. Columbia itself had a large number of free blacks, some quite prosperous, who helped the runaways.

From Columbia the escapees passed through Lancaster County on their way to Philadelphia. Many Lancaster County Quakers, and not a few Presbyterians, entered enthusiastically into the task of hiding the fugitives and passing them on from farm to farm. Other residents of the county were bitterly opposed to the underground railroad. They considered runaway slaves the legal property of the southerners. Neighbor against neighbor, brother against brother, the community took sides.

"What would thee think if thee had a horse stolen and taken to Maryland, and the person having him, knowing him to be stolen would refuse to give him up?" one conservative asked Jeremiah Moore, a Quaker active in the underground railroad.

"I would say to compare a man to a brute is unjust and unchristian," Jeremiah answered.

Although occasionally stirred by the visits of such famous antislavery lecturers as William Lloyd Garrison, the editor of the *Liberator,* the silver-tongued Abby Kelley, or the escaped slave Frederick Douglass, the abolitionists of Lancaster County were a down-to-earth lot, less interested in antislavery rhetoric than the day-to-day work of helping the escaping slaves. In this they were assisted by the Philadelphia Vigilance Committee, a black organization that helped several thousand slaves to escape from the South and eventually resettle in Canada. It kept in close touch with the movement of all escaped slaves in surrounding counties and warned black communities of the approach of posses and kidnappers. William Still, its director, freed almost as many of his fellow blacks as the famous Harriet Tubman.

Cooperation between the black resistance groups and the white abolitionists was usually good. For the pacifist Quakers, however, it sometimes raised special problems. They did not believe in the use of force under any circumstances. Should they urge the blacks not to resist the slave owners forcibly? But in that case should they not first convince the slave owners to give up the use of force? Most decided to carry on their side of the struggle nonviolently, but not to interfere with the blacks in their choice of method.

A good example of the cooperation of the Quaker abolitionists and the blacks occurred in 1828 when two slaveholders appeared one day in the field of a Quaker farmer, Truman Cooper, in lower Lancaster County, and seized an escaped slave who had been working on the farm for several years. Cooper was away at the time, but a young boy living on the farm saw the whole transaction and raced off on foot to notify the local abolitionists.

Mounting their fastest horses, these men galloped after the slaveholders until they caught up with them. Then, pretending to be merely casual passersby, they asked where the party planned to spend the night. The slave owners had no way of knowing these men were abolitionists, so they told them they were headed for a public tavern in Georgetown. The abolitionists rode leisurely on until they were out of sight, then galloped to Georgetown and informed the local black people that an escaped slave and his captors were on the way. The word spread quickly through the little community, and by nightfall the tavern was surrounded by an armed black group.

In due course the southerners arrived and called for dinner. While they were eating, the tavern owner's wife, herself an abolitionist, loosened the slave's handcuffs, and he managed to push open the door and flee. The slave owners rushed out to pursue him, but saw before them a phalanx of resolute blacks. While they stood there, uncertain what to do next, the slave raced away and then headed for the home of Jeremiah Moore in Sadsbury Township. Moore dressed him in a suit of Quaker gray, and sent him on his way through Chester County to Canada.

Sadsbury, on the easternmost border of Lancaster County, was in an ideal position to play a key role in the underground railroad. From here escapees could cross Chester and Delaware counties and so reach Philadelphia. Or they could cross Chester to Montgomery County and start north by way of Norristown. Because of its good connections, Sadsbury was the junction of two lines of the escape routes: one coming from Columbia and Lancaster and one cutting up from the Maryland border through the township of Little Brittany.

Bart Township, next to Sadsbury, also played a key role.

At about the time of the kidnapping of the fence and rail maker, a young black man named William Parker escaped from his slave owner in Maryland and took up residence first in Bart and then in Sadsbury Township. He was very young when he first arrived, but he was exceptionally intelligent, strong, and determined. Thomas Whitson, an abolitionist of Bart Township, once described him. "He was a dark mulatto of medium height, wonderfully muscled, and possessed of resolution, courage, and action. He could walk leisurely up to an ordinary post fence, leap over it without touching his hands, work hard all day, and travel ten to fifteen miles at night to organize his people."

At the time he lived in Lancaster County, Parker was illiterate. Nevertheless, he knew the Bible by heart and was able to outargue or outquote any adversary. He also won admiration as a devoted husband and father. Shortly after his arrival in Bart Township he married a young escaped slave, Eliza Howard, and together they had three children. Whenever possible he was home with his young family.

Within a year of his coming Parker had organized the blacks into a mutual defense network, pledged to fight before they would let any one of their number be kidnapped or taken back into slavery. For almost ten years he was the acknowledged leader in a series of daring rescues.

The Gap gang came to fear Parker, as the blacks feared William Baer. Although not a man prone to violence, Parker did not hesitate to use it when it seemed necessary to rescue a brother or sister. On one occasion he exchanged gunfire with a slave-catching posse. On another he boasted that he beat two men so badly that they later died. (These men must have been outlaws. Had they been respectable white citizens the whole nation would have been aroused by such an act.)

Parker sometimes felt it was necessary to use violence against his own people. Blacks as well as whites were tempted to play the role of informer for the sake of rewards. When Parker discovered that a black man was serving as an informer, he beat him up or burned down his house.

Although Parker's rescues and reprisals dismayed the kidnappers, the kidnapping did not stop. There was too much money in it. Instead, the Gap gang began to plan how to get Parker out of the way. At the same time southern slaveholders began to campaign for a more stringent fugitive slave law that would put an end to the underground railroad by punishing anyone, black or white, who interfered with the recapture of a slave. A time of crisis was approaching.

CHAPTER 2

PARKER'S ACCOUNT
He Comes to Lancaster County

WILLIAM PARKER'S OWN ACCOUNT OF HIS LIFE AND OF the events of the Christiana riot was published in 1866 in the February and March issues of the *Atlantic Monthly*. At the time Parker's account was published some people doubted that he was really the author, since he had started out as an illiterate slave. However, after Parker left Pennsylvania, he settled in an experimental community for escaped slaves in North Buxton, Ontario, Canada, and there learned to read and write so well that he held political office and became the correspondent for an antislavery newspaper, *The North Star*. Parker may have had some black collaboration in Buxton, but the editor who published Parker's manuscript in 1866 attested to the fact that he had given it only a slight editing. (In some cases Parker's spelling of proper names differs from other accounts of the period.)

I was born opposite to Queen Anne, in Anne Arundel County, in the State of Maryland, on a plantation called Rowdown. My master was Major

William [Brogdon], one of the wealthy men of that region. He had two sons, William, a doctor, and David, who held some office at Annapolis, and for some years was a member of the Legislature.

My old master died when I was very young; so I know little about him, except from statements received from my fellow-slaves, or casual remarks made in my hearing from time to time by white persons. From those I conclude that he was in no way peculiar, but should be classed with those slaveholders who are not remarkable either for the severity or the indulgence they extend to their people.

My mother, who was named Louisa Simms, died when I was very young; and to my grandmother I am indebted for the very little kindness I received in my early childhood; and this kindness could only be shown me at long intervals, and in a hurried way, as I shall presently show.

Like every Southern plantation of respectable extent and pretensions, our place had what is called the "Quarter," or place where the slaves of both sexes are lodged and fed. With us the Quarter was composed of a number of low buildings, with an additional building for single people and such of the children as were either orphans or had parents sold away or otherwise disposed of. This building was a hundred feet long by thirty wide, and had a large fireplace at either end, and small rooms arranged along the sides. In these rooms the children were huddled from day to day, the smaller and weaker subject to the whims and caprices of the larger and stronger. The largest children would always seize upon the warmest and best places, and say to us who were smaller, "Stand back, little chap, out of my way"; and we had to stand back or get a thrashing.

When my grandmother, who was cook at the "great house," came to look after me, she always brought me a morsel privately; and at such times I was entirely free from annoyance by the older ones. But as she could visit me only once in twenty-four hours, my juvenile days enjoyed but little rest from my domineering superiors in years and strength.

When my grandmother would inquire of the others how her "little boy" was getting on, they would tell her that I was doing well, and kindly invite me to the fire to warm myself. I was afraid to complain to her of their treatment as, for so doing, they would have beaten me, after she had gone to the "great house" again. I was thus compelled to submit to their misrepresentation, as well as to their abuse and indifference, until I grew older, when, by fighting first with one and then with another, I became "too many" for them, and could have a seat at the fire as well as the best. This experience of my boyhood has since been repeated in my manhood. My rights at the fireplace were won by my child-fists; my rights as a freeman were, under God, secured by my own right arm.

Old master had seventy slaves, mostly field-hands. My father was a fieldhand. He finally died;

but after that everything went on as usual for about six years, at the end of which time the brothers, David and William, divided the land and slaves. Then, with many others, including my brother and uncle, it fell to my lot to go with Master David, who built a house on the southeast part of the farm, and called it Nearo.

Over the hands at Nearo an overseer named Robert Brown was placed; but as he was liked by neither master nor slaves, he was soon discharged. The following circumstance led to his dismissal sooner, perhaps, than it would otherwise have happened.

While master was at Annapolis, my mistress, who was hard to please, fell out with one of the house-servants, and sent for Mr. Brown to come and whip her. When he came, the girl refused to be whipped, which angered Brown, and he beat her so badly that she was nearly killed before she gave up. When Master David came home, and saw the girl's condition, he became very angry, and turned Brown away at once.

Master David owned a colored man named Bob Wallace. He was a trusty man; and as he understood farming thoroughly, he was installed foreman in place of Brown. Everything went on very well for a while under Wallace, and the slaves were as contented as it is possible for slaves to be.

Neither of our young masters would allow his hands to be beaten or abused, as many slaveholders would; but every year they sold one or more of them—sometimes as many as six or seven at a time. One morning word was brought to the Quarter that we should not work that day, but go up to the "great house." As we were about obeying the summons, a number of strange white men rode up to

the mansion. They were negro-traders. Taking alarm, I ran away to the woods with a boy of about my own age, named Levi Storax; and there we remained until the selections for the sale were made, and the traders drove away. It was a serious time while they remained. Men, women, and children, all were crying, and general confusion prevailed. For years they had associated together in their rude way,—the old counseling the young, recounting their experience, and sympathizing in their trials; and now, without a word of warning, and for no fault of their own, parents and children, husbands and wives, brothers and sisters, were separated to meet no more on earth. A slave sale of this sort is always as solemn as a funeral and partakes of its nature in one important particular,—the meeting no more in the flesh.

Levi and I climbed a pine-tree, when we got to the woods, and had this conversation together.

"Le," I said to him, "our turn will come next; let us run away, and not be sold like the rest."

"If we can only get clear this time," replied Le, "may-be they won't sell us. I will go to Master William, and ask him not to do it."

"What will you get by going to Master William?" I asked him. "If we see him and ask him

· 20 ·

not to sell us, he will do as he pleases. For my part, I think the best thing is to run away to the Free States."

"But," replied Levi, "see how many start for the Free States and are brought back, and sold away down South. We could not be safe this side of Canada, and we should freeze to death before we got there."

So ended our conversation. I must have been about ten or eleven years old then; yet, young as I was, I had heard of Canada as the land far away in the North, where the runaway was safe from pursuit; but, to my imagination, it was a vast and cheerless waste of ice and snow. So the reader can readily conceive of the effect of Levi's remarks. They were a damper upon our flight for the time being.

When night came, Levi wanted to go home and see if they had sold his mother; but I did not care about going back, as I had no mother to sell. How desolate I was! No home, no protector, no mother, no attachments. As we turned our faces toward the Quarter,—where we might at any moment be sold to satisfy a debt or replenish a failing purse,—I felt myself to be what I really was, a poor, friendless slave-boy. Levi was equally sad. His mother was not sold, but she could afford him no protection.

To the question, "Where had we been?" we answered, "Walking around." Then followed inquiries and replies as to who were sold, who remained, and what transpired at the sale.

Said Levi,—

"Mother, were you sold?"

"No, child; but a good many were sold; among them, your Uncles Anthony and Dennis."

I said—

"Aunt Ruthy, did they sell Uncle Sammy?"

"No, child."

"Where, then, is Uncle Sammy?"

I thought, if I could be with Uncle Sammy, may-be I would be safe. My Aunt Rachel, and her two children, Jacob and Priscilla, were among the sold, who altogether comprised a large number of the servants.

The apologist for slavery at the North, and the owner of his fellow-man at the South, have steadily denied that the separation of families, except for punishment, was perpetrated by Southern masters; but my experience of slavery was, that separation by sale was a part of the system. Not only was it resorted to by severe masters, but, as in my own case, by those generally regarded as mild. No punishment was so much dreaded by the refractory slave as selling. The atrocities known to be committed on plantations in the Far South, tidings of which reached the slave's ears in various ways, his utter helplessness upon the best farms and under the most humane masters and overseers, in Maryland and other Northern Slave States, together with the impression that the journey was of great extent, and comfortless even to a slave, all combined to make a voyage down the river or down South an era in the life of the poor slave to which he looked forward with the most intense and bitter apprehension and anxiety.

This slave sale was the first I had ever seen. The next did not occur until I was thirteen years old; but every year, during the interval, one or more poor souls were disposed of privately.

Levi, my comrade, was one of those sold in this interval. Well may the good John Wesley speak of slavery as the sum of all villanies; for no resort is too despicable, no subterfuge too vile, for its supporters. Is a slave intractable, the most wicked punishment is not too severe; is he timid, obedient, attached to his birthplace and kindred, no lie is so base that it may not be used to entrap him into a change of place or of owners. Levi was made the victim of a stratagem so peculiarly Southern, and so thoroughly the outgrowth of an institution which holds the bodies and souls of men as of no more account, for all moral purposes, than the unreasoning brutes, that I cannot refrain from relating it. He was a likely lad, and, to all appearance, fully in the confidence of his master. Prompt and obedient, he seemed to some of us to enjoy high favor at the "great house." One morning he was told to take a letter to Mr. Henry Hall, an acquaintance of the family; and it being a part of his usual employment to bring and carry such missives, off he started, in blind confidence, to learn at the end of his journey that he had parted with par-

· 23 ·

ents, friends, and all, to find in Mr. Hall a new master. Thus, in a moment, his dearest ties were severed.

I met him about two months afterwards at the Cross-Road Meeting-House, on West River; and, after mutual recognition, I said to him,—

"Levi, why don't you come home?"

"I am at home," said he; "I was sold by Master William to Mr. Henry Hall."

He then told me about the deception practised upon him. I thought that a suitable opportunity to remind him of our conversation when up the pine-tree, years before, and said,—

"You told me, that, if you could escape the big sale, Master William would not sell you. Now you see how it was: the big sale was over, and yet you were sold to a worse master than you had before. I told you this would be so. The next time I hear from you, you will be sold again. Master Mack will be selling me one of these days, no doubt; but if he does, he will have to do it running."

Here ended our conversation and our association, as it was not in our power to meet afterward.

The neighbors generally called Master David, Mack, which was one of his Christian names; and the slaves called him Master Mack; so the reader will understand, that, whenever that name occurs, Master David is meant.

After the sale of Levi, I became greatly attached to Alexander Brown, another slave. Though not permitted to learn to read and write, and kept in profound ignorance of everything, save what belonged strictly to our plantation duties, we were not without crude perceptions of the dignity and independence belonging to freedom; and often, when out of hearing of the white people, or certain ones among our fellow-servants, Alexander and I would talk the subject over in our simple way.

Master Mack had a very likely young house-servant named Ann. She was between sixteen and eighteen years old; every one praised her intelligence and industry; but these commendable characteristics did not save her. She was sold next after Levi. Master told the foreman, Bob Wallace, to go to Annapolis, and take Ann with him. When Wallace told me he was going, I had a presentiment that the purpose was to sell the girl, and I told him so; but, man as he was, he had no fear about it. Wallace and Ann started for the city on horseback, and journeyed along pleasantly until they reached the town and were near the market-place, when a man came up to them, took Ann off the horse without ceremony, and put her into jail. Wallace, not suspecting the manoeuvre, attacked the man, and came well-nigh getting into difficulty. When Wallace returned, he said to Master Mack, "Why did you not tell me that Ann was sold, and not have me fighting for her? They might have put me in jail." But his master did not appear to hear him.

Poor Uncle Henry followed Ann. His wife lived in Annapolis, and belonged to a Mr. George Mc-

Near, residing there. Uncle Henry went one Saturday night to see her, when Master William put him into jail for sale; and that was the last we saw or heard of him.

Parker's Account

Alex Brown's mother followed next. After the poor woman was gone, I said to Alex,—

"Now that your mother has been sold, it is time that you and I studied out a plan to run away and be free."

But so thoroughly had his humanity been crushed by the foul spirit of Slavery, so apathetic had he—though in the vigor of youth—become from long oppression, that he would not agree to my suggestion.

"No," he said, " 't is no use for you and I to run away. It is too far to the Free States. We could not get there. They would take us up and sell us; so we had better not go. Master Mack can't sell any more of his hands; there are no more than can carry on his farm."

"Very well," said I, "trust to that, and you will see what will come of it."

After that I said no more to him, but determined to be free. My brother Charles was of like mind; but we kept our thoughts to ourselves. How old I was then I do not know; but from what the neighbors told me, I must have been about seventeen. Slaveholders are particular to keep the pedigree and age of favorite horses and dogs, but are quite indifferent about the age of their servants, until they want to purchase. Then they are careful to select young persons, though not one in twenty can tell year, month, or day. Speaking of births,—it is the time of "corn planting," "corn-husking," "Christmas," "New Year," "Easter," "the Fourth of July," or some similar indefinite date. My own time of birth was no more exact; so that to this day I am uncertain how old I am.

About the time of the conversation last narrated, Jefferson Dorsey, a planter near by, had a butchering. One of Dorsey's men met me, and said that they wanted more help, and that Master Mack said I might go and lend a hand. Thinking that he spoke truth, I did not ask permission, but went, and stayed until noon. I soon learned, however, that the man had deceived me.

Master Mack, when told by some of the people where I was, sent my brother John after me, with the threat of a whipping. On reaching home, the women also told me that master would almost kill me. This excited me greatly, and I replied,—

"Master Mack is 'most done whipping me."

When I went in to see him, I saw plainly enough that his face foretold a storm.

"Boy," said he, "yoke up the oxen, and haul a load of wood."

I went at once, and did the task; but, to my dismay, there he stood at the stable. I had to drive near to him; and as he evidently intended to catch me, I was all vigilance.

"When you unload that wood, come to me, Sir," he said.

I made no reply, but unloaded the wood, left the oxen standing, and stole away to Dorsey's, where I staid until the next day. Then I prevailed upon Samuel Dorsey to go home with me. Master Mack told me to go to my work, and he would forgive me; but the next time he would pay me for "the new and the old." To work I went; but I determined not to be paid for "the new and the old."

Parker's Account

This all occurred in the month of May. Everything went on well until June, when the long-sought-for-opportunity presented itself. I had been making preparations to leave ever since Master Mack had threatened me; yet I did not like to go without first having a difficulty with him. Much as I disliked my condition, I was ignorant enough to think that something besides the fact that I was a slave was necessary to exonerate me from blame in running away. A cross word, a blow, a good fright, anything, would do, it mattered not whence nor how it came. I told my brother, Charles, who shared my confidence, to be ready; for the time was at hand when we should leave Old Maryland forever. I was only waiting for the first crooked word from my master.

A few days afterwards all hands were ordered to the fields to work; but I stayed behind, lurking about the house. I was tired of working without pay. Master Mack saw me, and wanted to know why I did not go out. I answered, that it was raining, that I was tired, and did not want to work. He then picked up a stick used for an ox-goad, and said, if I did not go to work, he would whip me as sure as there was a God in heaven. Then he struck at me, but I caught the stick, and we grappled, and handled each other roughly for a time, when he called for assistance. He was badly hurt. I let go my hold, bade him good-bye, and ran for the woods. As I went by the field, I beckoned to my brother, who left work, and joined me at a rapid pace.

I was now at the beginning of a new and important era in my life. Although upon the threshold of manhood, I had, until the relation with my master was sundered, only dim perceptions of the responsibilities of a more independent position. I longed to cast off the chains of servitude, because they chafed my free spirit, and because I had a notion that my position was founded in injustice; but it has only been since a struggle of many years, and indeed, since I settled upon British soil, that I have realized fully the grandeur of my position as a free man.

One fact, when I was a slave, often filled me with indignation. There were many poor white lads of about my own age, belonging to families scattered around, who were as poor in personal effects as we were; and yet, though our companions, (when we chose to tolerate them,) they did not have to be controlled by a master, to go and come at his command, to be sold for his debts, or whenever he wanted extra pocketmoney. The preachers of a slave-trading gospel frequently told us, in their sermons, that we should be "good boys," and not break into master's henroost, nor steal his bacon; but they never told this to these poor white people, although they knew very well that they encouraged the slaves to steal, trafficked in stolen goods, and stole themselves.

Why this difference? I felt I was the equal of these poor whites, and naturally I concluded that we were greatly wronged, and that all this talk about obedience, duty, humility, and honesty was, in the phrase of my companions, "all gammon."

But I was now on the high-road to liberty. I had broken the bonds that held me so firmly; and now, instead of fears of recapture, that before had haunted my imagination whenever I thought of running away, I felt as light as a feather, and seemed to be helped onward by an irresistible force.

Some time before this, I had been able, through the instrumentality of a friend, to procure a pass, for which I paid five dollars,—all the money I had saved in a long time; but as my brother determined to go with me, and as we could not both use it safely, I destroyed it.

On the day I ceased working for master, after gaining the woods, we lurked about and discussed our plans until after dark. Then we stole back to the Quarter, made up our bundles, bade some of our friends farewell, and at about nine o'clock of the night set out for Baltimore. How shall I describe my first experience of free life? Nothing can be greater than the contrast it affords to a plantation experience, under the suspicious and vigilant eye of a mercenary overseer or a watchful master. Day and night are not more unlike. The mandates of Slavery are like leaden sounds, sinking with dead weight into the very soul, only to deaden and destroy. The impulse of freedom lends wings to the feet, buoys up the spirit within, and the fugitive catches glorious glimpses of light through rifts and seams in the accumulated ignorance of his years of oppression. How briskly we travelled on that eventful night and the next day!

We reached Baltimore on the following evening, between seven and eight o'clock. When we neared the city, the patrols were out, and the difficulty was to pass them unseen or unsuspected. I learned of a brick-yard at the entrance to the city; and thither we went at once, took brick-dust and threw it up on our clothes, hats, and boots, and then walked on. Whenever we met a passer-by, we would brush off some of the dust, and say aloud, "Boss gave us such big tasks, we would leave him. We ought to have been in a long time before." By this ruse we reached quiet quarters without arrest or suspicion.

We remained in Baltimore a week, and then set out for Pennsylvania.

We started with the brightest visions of future independence; but soon they were suddenly dimmed by one of those unpleasant incidents which annoy the fugitive at every step of his onward journey.

The first place at which we stopped to rest was a

village on the old York road, called New Market. There nothing occurred to cause us alarm; so, after taking some refreshments, we proceeded towards York; but when near Logansville, we were interrupted by three white men, one of whom, a very large man, cried,—

"Hallo!"

I answered,—

"Hallo to you!"

"Which way are you travelling?" he asked.

We replied,—

"To Little York."

"Why are you travelling so late?"

"We are not later than you are," I answered.

"Your business must be of consequence," he said.

"It is. We want to go to York to attend to it; and if you have any business, please attend to it, and don't be meddling with ours on the public highway. We have no business with you, and I am sure you have none with us."

"See here!" said he; "you are the fellows that this advertisement calls for," at the same time taking the paper out of his pocket, and reading it to us.

Sure enough, there we were, described exactly. He came closely to us, and said,—

"You must go back."

I replied,—

"If I must, I must, and you must take me."

"Oh, you need not make any big talk about it," he answered; "for I have taken back many a runaway, and I can take you. What's that you have in your hand?"

"A stick."

He put his hand into his pocket, as if to draw a pistol, and said,—

"Come! give up your weapons."

I said again,—

" 'T is only a stick."

He then reached for it, when I stepped back and struck him a heavy blow on the arm. It fell as if broken; I think it was. Then he turned and ran, and I after him. As he ran, he would look back over his shoulder, see me coming, and then run faster, and halloo with all his might. I could not catch him, and it seemed, that, the longer he ran, the faster he went. The other two took to their heels at the first alarm,—thus illustrating the valor of the chivalry!

At last I gave up the chase. The whole neighborhood by that time was aroused, and we thought best to retrace our steps to the place whence we started. Then we took a roundabout course until we reached the railroad, along which we travelled. For a long distance there was unusual stir and commotion. Every house was lighted up; and we heard people talking and horses galloping this way and that way, with other evidences of unusual excitement. This was between one and two o'clock in the morning. We walked on a long distance before we lost the sounds; but about four o'clock the same morning entered York, where we remained during the day.

Once in York, we thought we should be safe, but were mistaken. A similar mistake is often made by fugitives. Not accustomed to travelling, and unacquainted with the facilities for communication, they think that a few hours' walk is a long journey, and foolishly suppose, that if they have few opportunities of knowledge, their masters can have none at all at such great distances. But our ideas of security were materially lessened when we met with a friend during the day, who advised us to proceed farther, as we were not out of imminent danger.

Parker's
Account

According to this advice we started that night for Columbia. Going along in the dark, we heard persons following. We went very near to the fence that they might pass without observing us. There were two, apparently in earnest conversation. The one who spoke so as to be distinctly heard we discovered to be Master Mack's brother-in-law. He remarked to his companion that they must hurry and get to the bridge before we crossed. He knew that we had not gone over yet. We were then near enough to have killed them, concealed as we were by the darkness; but we permitted them to pass unmolested, and went on to Wrightsville that night.

The next morning we arrived at Columbia before it was light, and fortunately without crossing the bridge, for we were taken over in a boat. At Wrightsville we met a woman with whom we were before acquainted, and our meeting was very gratifying. We there inclined to halt for a time.

I was not used to living in town, and preferred a home in the country; so to the country we decided to go. After resting for four days, we started towards Lancaster to try to procure work. I got a place about five miles from Lancaster, and then set to work in earnest.

While a slave, I was, as it were, groping in the dark, no ray of light penetrating the intense gloom surrounding me. My scanty garments felt too tight for me, my very respiration seemed to be restrained by some supernatural power. Now, free as I supposed, I felt like a bird on a pleasant May morning. Instead of the darkness of slavery, my eyes were almost blinded by the light of freedom.

Those were memorable days, and yet much of this was boyish fancy. After a few years of life in a Free State, the enthusiasm of the lad materially sobered down, and I found, by bitter experience, that to preserve my stolen liberty I must pay, unremittingly, an almost sleepless vigilance; yet to this day I have never looked back regretfully to Old Maryland, nor yearned for her flesh-pots.

I have said I engaged to work; I hired my services for three months for the round sum of three dollars per month. I thought this was an immense sum. Fast work was no trouble to me; for when the work was done, the money was mine. That was a great consideration. I could go out on Saturdays and Sundays, and home when I pleased, without being whipped. I thought of my fellow-servants left behind, bound in the chains of slavery,—and I was free! I thought, that, if I had the power, they should soon be as free as I was; and I formed a resolution that I would assist in liberating every one within my reach at the risk of my life, and that I would devise some plan for their entire liberation.

My brother went about fifteen miles farther on, and also got employment. I "put in" three months with my employer, "lifted" my wages, and then went to visit my brother. He lived in Bart Township, near Smyrna; and after my visit was over, I engaged to work for a Dr. Dengy, [Dingee], living near by. I remained with him thirteen months. I never have been better treated than by the Doctor; I liked him and the family, and they seemed to think well of me.

CHAPTER 3

---•---

The New Fugitive Slave Law

O N THE NIGHT OF OCTOBER 11, 1850, A GROUP OF Lancaster County abolitionists met at the Bart Township schoolhouse to protest the new Fugitive Slave Law passed by Congress in late September after a long and bitter fight. The new law was specifically designed to end the underground railroad. It provided that if a person tried to conceal or rescue an escaped slave, he was fined a thousand dollars or given six months in jail. Worse yet, United States marshals and special commissioners, appointed under the law to help slave owners catch up with their runaway property, had the right to demand of any innocent bystander that he assist in the capture.

The abolitionists had no intention of obeying this new law. They pledged themselves on the spot to continue to "harbor, feed and aid the escape of fugitives in opposition to the law." But they were especially worried and angered by the provision that any citizen must help the slave owner. What would this do to their neighbors who had taken no stand on the issue of slavery? Turn them into allies of the slave catchers? Set neighbor against neighbor? That new miller at the brick mill up the valley in Sadsbury Township, for instance. What would he do?

The slave owners had always had the law on their side. The United States Constitution itself protected their right to recover runaway slaves who sought refuge in other states. An original Fugitive Slave Law passed in 1793 reinforced this constitutional provision. (When some of the northern states, including Pennsylvania, passed laws forbidding state law enforcement officers to help in the recapture, the United States Supreme Court ruled that such laws were unconstitutional.) Nevertheless, because of northern sympathy for the escaping slaves, the original law had proved hard to enforce. This new one, tougher and more coercive, represented a last ditch effort on the part of southerners and the federal government to end once and for all the practice of aiding the runaways.

All over the North abolitionists were holding protest meetings. They were not only angry about the new law; they felt its passage represented defeat. The Fugitive Slave Law was part of a series of congressional decisions called the Compromise of 1850. Like most compromises, it pleased practically nobody, although it managed to hold the Union together for another ten shaky years.

Impetus for the Compromise of 1850 came when California applied for admission to the United States as a free state. Up until this time Congress had carefully kept the balance even between slave and free states by admitting first a free state, then a slave state. California would upset that balance. Its admission came at a time when southerners were particularly angry about the activities of the underground railroad, and the increasingly strident propaganda of the abolitionists, some of whom were calling for slave rebellion. Southern landowners began to feel they would be better off in a slave-owning republic stretching from the Potomac to the Pacific than in a union over which they had lost voting control and which failed to protect the investment they had made in slaves. Throughout the South talk of secession grew.

Northern statesmen, such as Daniel Webster from Massachusetts, and southern statesmen, such as Henry Clay of Kentucky, were determined to hold the Union together. It was Clay in January of 1850 who introduced into Congress a set of resolutions that formed the backbone of the compromise. In addition to the new fugitive slave law, the Compromise of 1850 called for the admission of California as a free state, gave Utah and New Mexico the choice of being either slave or free when they were admitted, and abolished the slave trade, but not slavery itself, in the District of Columbia.

The abolitionists were not pleased. They did not want to see slavery extended to *any* new territories, and they thought it was a disgrace that it continued in the nation's capital. As for the southerners, the only good they saw in the compromise was the new and more effective fugitive slave law. They were, therefore, determined to make its enforcement the test of the whole compromise. If the new law was strictly enforced, they would consider remaining in the Union. If not, they would likely secede.

Northern blacks saw the new law in personal terms. One of its provisions created special United States commissioners to enforce the return of slaves and paid them on a fee basis. They were to receive ten dollars every time they ruled in favor of a slave owner, but only five dollars when they ruled against him. This was going to make it far more profitable to catch slaves than to let them go. The law would also prevent many white farmers from continuing to offer shelter to escaping slaves, and would force bystanders to join in their pursuit. No, the blacks reasoned, from now on their safety, and that of their brothers and sisters, rested solely on themselves.

In many communities, therefore, the blacks organized as they had in Lancaster County under William Parker. The first attempts to enforce the Fugitive Slave Law were met with determined black resistance, and the first dramatic slave rescues were conducted by the blacks themselves.

On October 8, 1850, just a few weeks after the passage of the new law, a black man was arrested in Detroit as a runaway. Immediately several hundreds of armed blacks gathered to rescue the prisoner. Federal troops were quickly brought in to protect him as he was taken from the jail to the courthouse. Still the crowd outside grew. Alarmed, the slave owner agreed to sell the man to a group of local abolitionists, black and white, for only five hundred dollars. Since he had spent two hundred dollars having the man arrested and brought to trial, he was left with a balance of only three hundred dollars for a thousand dollar slave. He went South again, a poorer but wiser man.

The most sensational slave rescue of the period came a few months later. In February 1851, Frederick Jenkins, nicknamed Shadrack, was arrested in Boston where he worked as a waiter at a coffeehouse. Rather than being placed in jail overnight, Shadrack was taken immediately to the courtroom for a hearing before the commissioner. Several prominent abolitionist lawyers promptly offered to take the case, but said they needed time to prepare the defense. They asked the commissioner for a three-day delay.

The commissioner agreed, and the courtroom was cleared except for the marshals, one black lawyer, and Shadrack himself, who was sitting unshackled between two officers. Suddenly a mob of blacks burst into the courtroom, seized Shadrack, and made off with him under the very eyes of the startled marshals. It was all so quick that before anyone could do anything, Shadrack was free and galloping away from Boston en route to Canada. He settled in Montreal, married an Irish woman, and opened an eating house.

Four blacks and four whites were indicted for assisting in Shadrack's rescue, but the Boston jury, which was sympathetic to him, did not feel there was adequate proof against the rescuers, and all were let go unpunished. The southern papers were full of wrath. The verdict made it clear that the United States government was not going to enforce the new Fugitive Slave Law after all. Abolitionists, both black and white, on the other hand, were joyful. It seemed they had won an important victory. Just a few months later, however, they suffered a defeat when an attempt to rescue another slave, Thomas Sims, in Boston, met with failure.

These cases, widely reported in antislavery newspapers, were read with avid interest in Lancaster County. Those blacks who could read described the events to those who could not. Abolitionists, both black and white, longed for a chance to prove their courage equal to that reported in the newspapers.

Shortly before the Shadrack rescue, the people of Sadsbury Township were shocked, outraged, and saddened by the most brutal case of kidnapping ever undertaken by the Gap gang. One day in January 1851, a group of men approached the home of a farmer named Marsh Chamberlain who lived on the back road from Christiana to Gap, and told Marsh's son to say that they wanted to see his father because they were interested in buying some chickens. Marsh invited them to stand on the porch while they were discussing the transaction, and one of them glanced through the window and saw a black man sitting by the stove. After about ten minutes they left, and the family was just getting settled down for the evening when a neighbor ran up, out of breath, to report that a local farmer had fallen dead as he entered his own house, and Marsh was needed to help in the emergency.

Marsh hurried off to the bereaved home, leaving his father-in-law, Thomas Penington, sitting downstairs with the black man, John Williams. Marsh's wife and children were upstairs getting ready for bed. About a half hour later a man knocked on the door, then six men entered the kitchen without invitation, and put a pistol to John Williams' head. John attempted to defend himself, and there followed a struggle, in the course of which someone knocked over a lamp. Marsh Chamberlain's wife, who was watching the whole affair through a heat register in the floor above, came partway downstairs and begged her old father to come with her before he was hurt. Returning to the air vent, the two watched while John was overpowered and dragged off, after being given a savage beating. Later, when Marsh returned, they were able to trace John's path by a heavy trail of blood.

Called to the rescue, William Parker followed the kidnappers and their mutilated cargo all the way to the Maryland border. Farther than that he dared not go. Later the Chamberlain family learned that John was so badly injured that the man who claimed to be his owner refused to give the Gap gang the reward he had promised them. However, after some months, Williams recovered enough to be sold South to a cotton gang, and William Baer and Perry Marsh got their money.

Immediately after this occurrence the local abolitionists, including Moses Whitson, Samuel Whitson, Samuel Brinton, Lindley Coates, John Cain, and Dr. Augustus Cain, met with lawyer and abolitionist Thomas Earle to see if a case could be brought against Baer for kidnapping. Earle discouraged them. They had no way of proving that the man had not been returned to his rightful owner, though the manner of arrest was unusual. Under the new law nothing could be done.

The Gap gang in turn now resolved to punish the

abolitionists for their efforts to interfere. Three of the party who had wanted to prosecute Baer for kidnapping were warned that their barns would be burned shortly. Samuel Whitson and Lindley Coates in fact saw their barns go up in flames that summer, but Dr. Cain kept a guard around his for two months and it escaped damage.

Shortly after the Williams kidnapping, Mary Ann Fulton, the daughter of a Sadsbury Township abolitionist farmer, had her first experience in being responsible for the operation of the underground railroad. A slave arrived at Joseph Fulton's farm and asked to be hidden because he was being hotly pursued. Joseph was out of town, so Mary Ann herself hid the man in the barn, bringing him food once every twenty-four hours. She did not speak to him, or let him speak to her, for fear someone might be listening, but tapped three times on the partition behind which he was hiding, and then withdrew.

At the end of the week, after her father returned, it was decided it would be safe to let the man continue on his journey toward freedom. Mary Ann gave him a map of Binghamton, New York, and a compass, and told him to travel only by night. Some weeks later she had a letter announcing that he had arrived safely and had found a job. This experience prepared her to play an important role in the great adventure that lay ahead.

The summer of 1851 was long and hot in Sadsbury Township. Outwardly peaceful with its great fields of corn and potatoes, the area sputtered and crackled with tension.

CHAPTER 4

PARKER'S ACCOUNT
The Defense Is Organized

ONE DAY, WHILE LIVING AT DR. DENGY'S [DINGEE'S], I was working in the barn-yard, when a man came to the fence, and, looking at me intently, went away. The Doctor's son, observing him, said,—

"Parker, that man, from his movements, must be a slaveholder or kidnapper. This is the second time he has been looking at you. If not a kidnapper, why does he look so steadily at you and not tell his errand?"

I said,—

"The man must be a fool! If he should come back and not say anything to me, I shall say something to him."

We then looked down the road and saw him coming again. He rode up to the same place and halted. I then went to the fence, and, looking him steadily in the eye, said,—

"Am I your slave?"

He made no reply, but turned his horse and rode off, at full speed, towards the valley. We did not see him again; but that same evening word was brought that kidnappers were in the valley, and if we were not careful, they would "hook" some of us. This caused a great excitement among the colored people of the neighborhood.

Parker's Account

A short while prior to this, a number of us had formed an organization for mutual protection against slaveholders and kidnappers, and had resolved to prevent any of our brethren being taken back into slavery, at the risk of our own lives. We collected together that evening, and went down to the valley; but the kidnappers had gone. We watched for them several nights in succession, without result; for so much alarmed were the tavern-keepers by our demonstration, that they refused to let them stop over night with them. Kidnapping was so common, while I lived with the Doctor, that we were kept in constant fear. We would hear of slaveholders or kidnappers every two or three weeks; sometimes a party of white men would break into a house and take a man away, no one knew where; and, again, a whole family would be carried off. There was no power to protect them, nor prevent it. So completely roused were my feelings, that I vowed to let no slaveholder take back a fugitive, if I could but get my eye on him.

One day word was sent to me that slaveholders had taken William Dorsey, and had put him into Lancaster jail to await a trial. Dorsey had a wife and three or four children; but what was it to the slaveholder, if the wife and children should starve? We consulted together, as to what course to take to deliver him; but no plan that was proposed could be worked. At last we separated, determining to get him away some way or other on the day of trial. His case caused great excitement. We attended the trial, and eagerly watched all the movements from an outside position, and had a man to tell us how proceedings were going on within. He finally came out and said that the case would go against Dorsey. We then formed in a column at the court-house door, and when the slaveholders and Dorsey came out, we walked close to them,—behind and around them,—trying to separate them from him. Before we had gone far towards the jail, a slaveholder drew a pistol on William Hopkins, one of our party. Hopkins defied him to shoot; but he did not. Then the slaveholder drew the pistol on me, saying, he would blow my black brains out, if I did not go away. I doubled my fists to knock him down, but some person behind caught my hand; this started a fracas, and we got Dorsey loose; but he was so confused that he stood stock still, until they tied him again. A general fight followed. Bricks, stones, and sticks fell in showers. We fought across the road and back again, and I thought our brains would be knocked out; when the whites, who were too numerous for us, commenced making arrests. They got me fast several times, but I succeeded in getting away. One of our men was arrested, and afterwards stood trial; but they did not convict him. Dorsey was put into jail, but was afterwards bought and liberated by friends.

My friends now said that I had got myself into a bad difficulty, and that my arrest would follow.

In this they were mistaken. I never was disturbed because of it, nor was the house at which I lodged ever searched, although the neighbors were repeatedly annoyed in that way. I distinctly remember that this was the second time that resistance had been made to their wicked deeds. Whether the kidnappers were clothed with legal authority or not, I did not care to inquire, as I never had faith in nor respect for the Fugitive-Slave Law.

The whites of that region were generally such negro-haters, that it was a matter of no moment to them where fugitives were carried,—whether to Lancaster, Harrisburg, or elsewhere.

The insolent and overbearing conduct of the Southerners, when on such errands to Pennsylvania, forced me to my course of action. They did not hesitate to break open doors, and to enter, without ceremony, the houses of colored men; and when refused admission, or when a manly and determined spirit was shown, they would present pistols, and strike and knock down men and women indiscriminately.

I was sitting one evening in a friend's house, conversing about these marauding parties, when I remarked to him that a stop should be put to such "didos," and declared, that, the next time a slaveholder came to a house where I was, I would refuse to admit him. His wife replied, "It will make a fuss." I told her, "It is time a fuss was made." She insisted that it would cause trouble, and it was best to let them alone and have peace. Then I told her we must have trouble before we could have peace. "The first slaveholder that draws a pistol on me I shall knock down."

We were interrupted, just at this stage of the conversation, by some one rapping at the door.

"Who's there?" I asked.

"It's me! Who do you think? Open the door!" was the response, in a gruff tone.

"What do you want?" I asked.

Without replying, the man opened the door and came in, followed by two others.

The first one said,—

"Have you any niggers here?"

"What have we to do with your niggers?" said I.

After bandying a few words, he drew his pistol upon me. Before he could bring the weapon to bear, I seized a pair of heavy tongs, and struck him a violent blow across the face and neck, which knocked him down. He lay for a few minutes senseless, but afterwards rose, and walked out of the house without a word, followed by his comrades, who also said nothing to us, but merely asked their leader, as they went out, if he was hurt.

The part of Lancaster County in which I lived was near Chester County. Not far away, in the latter county, lived Moses Whitson, a well-known Abolitionist, and a member of the Society of

Friends. Mr. Whitson had a colored girl living in his family, who was pounced upon by the slaveholders, awhile after the Dorsey arrest. About daylight three men went to Mr. Whitson's house and

told him that the girl he had living with him was their property, and that they intended to have her. Friend Whitson asked the girl if she knew any of the men, and if any of them was her master. She said, "No!" One of the slaveholders said he could prove that she was his property; and then they forcibly tied her, put her into a carriage, and started for Maryland.

While the kidnappers were contending with Moses Whitson for the girl, Benjamin Whipper, a colored man, who now lives in this country, sounded the alarm, that "the kidnappers were at Whitson's, and were taking away his girl." The news soon reached me, and with six or seven others, I followed them. We proceeded with all speed to a place called the Gap-Hill, where we overtook them, and took the girl away. Then we beat the kidnappers, and let them go. We learned afterwards that they were all wounded badly, and that two of them died in Lancaster, and the other did not get home for some time. Only one of our men was hurt, and he had only a slight injury in the hand.

Dr. Duffield and Squire Henderson, two respectable citizens of the town, were looking on during this entire engagement; and after we had stopped firing, they went up to the slaveholders, and the following conversation took place:—

Squire Henderson. What's the matter?

Slaveholder. You may ask, what's the matter! Is this the way you allow your niggers to do?

Squire. Why did you not shoot them?

Slaveholder. We did shoot at them, but it did not take effect.

Squire. There's no use shooting at our niggers, for their heads are like iron pots; the balls will glance off. What were you doing?

Slaveholder. Taking our property, when the niggers jumped on us and nearly killed some of the men.

Squire. Men coming after such property ought to be killed.

Slaveholder. Do you know where we can find a doctor?

Squire. Yes; there are plenty of doctors South.

Being much disabled, and becoming enraged, they abruptly left, and journeyed on until they reached McKenzie's tavern, where their wounds were dressed and their wants attended to. So strongly was McKenzie in sympathy with these demons, that he declared he would never employ another nigger, and actually discharged a faithful colored woman who had lived a long time in his employ. Dr. Lemmon, a physician on the road to Lancaster, refused to attend the slaveholders; so that by the time they got to the city, from being so long without surgical aid, their limbs were past setting, and two of them died, as before stated, while the other survived but a short time after reaching Maryland.

A large reward was offered by the Maryland authorities for the perpetrators of the flogging, but without effect.

McKenzie, the tavern-keeper referred to, boasted after this that he would entertain all slave-holders who came along, and help them recapture their slaves. We were equally determined he should not, if we could prevent it.

The following affliction was eventually the means, under Providence, by which he was led to adopt other views, and become a practical Abolitionist.

A band of five men stood off, one dark night, and saw with evident satisfaction the curling flames ascend above his barn, from girder to roof, and lap and lash their angry tongues in wild license, until every vestige of the building was consumed.

After that mysterious occurrence, the poor fugitive had no better friend than the publican McKenzie.

Shortly after the incidents just related, I was married to Eliza Ann Elizabeth Howard, a fugitive, whose experience of slavery had been much more bitter than my own. We commenced house-keeping, renting a room from Enoch Johnson for one month. We did not like our landlord, and when the time was up left, and rented a house of Isaac

Walker for one year. After the year was out, we left Walker's and went to Smyrna, and there I rented a house from Samuel D. Moore for another year. After the year was out we left Smyrna also, and went to Joseph Moore's to live. We lived on his place about five years. While we were living there, several kidnappers came into the neighborhood. On one occasion, they took a colored man and started for Maryland. Seven of us set out in pursuit, and, soon getting on their track, followed them to a tavern on the Westchester road, in Chester County. Learning that they were to remain for the night, I went to the door and asked for admittance. The landlord demanded to know if we were white or colored. I told him colored. He then told us to be gone, or he would blow out our brains. We walked aside a little distance, and consulted about what we should do. Our men seemed to dread the undertaking; but I told them we could overcome them, and that I would go in. One of them said he would follow at the risk of his life. The other five said we should all get killed,—that we were men with families,—that our wives and children needed our assistance,—and that they did not think we would be doing our families justice by risking our lives for one man. We two then went back to the tavern, and, after rapping, were told again by the landlord to clear out, after he found that we were colored. I pretended that we wanted something to drink. He put his head out of the window, and threatened again to shoot us; when my comrade raised his gun and would have shot him down, had I not caught his arm and persuaded him not to fire. I told the landlord that we wanted to come in and intended to come in. Then I went to the yard, got

a piece of scantling, took it to the door, and, by battering with it a short time, opened it. As soon as the door flew open, a kidnapper shot at us, and the ball lodged in my ankle, bringing me to the ground. But I soon rose, and my comrade then firing on them, they took to their heels. As they ran away, I heard one say, "We have killed one of them."

My companion and I then rushed into the house. We unbound the man, took him out, and started for home; but had hardly crossed the door-sill before people from the neighboring houses began to fire on us. At this juncture, our other five came up, and we all returned the compliment. Firing on both sides was kept up for ten or fifteen minutes, when the whites called for quarter, and offered to withdraw, if we would stop firing. On this assurance we started off with the man, and reached home safely.

The next day my ankle was very painful. With a knife I extracted the ball, but kept the wound secret; as long before we had learned that for our own security it was best not to let such things be generally known.

About ten o'clock of a Sabbath night, awhile after the event last narrated, we were aroused by the cry of "Kidnappers! kidnappers!" and immediately some one halloed under my window,—

"William! William!"

I put my head out and demanded his errand. He said,—

"Come here!"

I answered,—

"You must be a fool to think I am going to you at this time of the night, without knowing who you are and what you want."

He would not satisfy me, so I took my gun, and went out to him. I was then informed that kidnappers had been at Allen Williams's; that they had taken Henry Williams, and gone toward Maryland. I called one of our party, who dressed and proceeded to arouse our men. Two of us then started for the Nine Points, in Lancaster County, and left instructions for the other men to meet us in the valley. They did so, and we hurried on to our destination. We had not gone far before we heard some one calling, "Kidnappers! kidnappers!" Going back some distance, we found the cry came from a man who had fallen into a lime quarry. He was in a bad situation, and unable to get out without assistance, and, hearing us pass, concluded we were kidnappers and raised the cry. We were delayed for a time in helping him out, and it provoked me very much, as it was important we should be in haste.

We started again for the Nine Points, but, arriving there, learned to our dismay, that the kidnappers had passed an hour before. The chase was given up, but with saddened feelings. A fellow-being had been dragged into hopeless bondage, and we, his comrades, held our liberty as insecurely as he had done but a few short hours before! We asked ourselves the question, "Whose turn will come next?" I was delegated to find out, if possible, who had betrayed him, which I accordingly did.

Parker's Account

Lynch law is a code familiar to the colored people of the Slave States. It is of so diabolical a character as to be without justification, except when enforced by men of pure motives, and then only in extreme cases, as when the unpunished party has it in his power to barter away the lives and liberties of those whose confidence he possesses, and who would, by bringing him before a legal tribunal, expose themselves to the same risks that they are liable to from him. The frequent attacks from slaveholders and their tools, the peculiarity of our position, many being escaped slaves, and the secrecy attending these kidnapping exploits, all combined to make an appeal to the Lynch Code in our case excusable, if not altogether justifiable. Ourselves, our wives, our little ones, were insecure, and all we had was liable to seizure. We felt that something must be done, for some one must be in our midst with whom the slaveholders had communication. I inquired around, quietly, and soon learned that Allen Williams, the very man in whose house the fugitive was, had betrayed him. This information I communicated to our men. They met at my house and talked the matter over, and, after most solemnly weighing all the facts and evidence, we resolved that he should die, and we set about executing our purpose that evening. The difficulty was, how to punish him. Some were for shooting him, but this was not feasible. I proposed another plan, which was agreed to.

Accordingly, we went to his house and asked if a man named Carter, who lived with him, was at home, as rumor said that he had betrayed Henry Williams. He denied it, and said that Carter had fought for Henry with him, but the slaveholders being too strong for them, they had to give him up. He kept beyond reach, and the men apologized for intruding upon him, while I stepped up to the door and asked for a glass of water. He gave it to me, and to the others. When he was giving water to one of the party, I caught him by the throat, to prevent his giving the alarm, and drew him over my head and shoulders. Then the rest beat him until we thought we heard some one coming, which caused us to flee. If we had not been interrupted, death would have been his fate. At that time I was attending a threshing-machine for George Whitson and Joseph Scarlot [Scarlett].

It must have been a month after the Williams affray, that I was sitting at home one evening talking with Pinckney and Samuel Thompson about how I was getting on with my work, when I thought I heard some one call my name. I went out, but all was quiet. When I went in, Pinckney and Thompson laughed at me, and said that I had become so "scary" that I could not stay in the house. But I was not satisfied. I was sure some one had called me. I said so, and that I would go to Marsh Chamberlain's to see if anything was wrong. They concluded to go also, and we started.

Arriving near the house, I told Pinckney and Thompson to stop outside, and I would go in, and if anything was wrong, would call them. When I reached the house, I saw a chair broken to pieces, and knew that something had happened. I said,—

"Hallo, Marsh!"

"Who is that?" said he.

And his wife said,—

"Parker, is that you?"

"Yes," I said.

"Oh, Parker, come here!" she called.

I called Pinckney and Thompson, and we went in. Marsh met us, and said that kidnappers had been there, had taken John Williams, and gone with him towards Buck Hill. They had then been gone about fifteen minutes. Off we started on a rapid run to save him. We ran to a stable, got out two horses, and Pinckney and I rode on. Thompson soon got the rest of our party together and followed. We were going at a pretty good gait, when Pinckney's horse stumbled and fell, fastening his rider's leg; but I did not halt. Pinckney got his horse up and caught up with me.

"You would not care," said he, "if a man were to get killed! You would not help him!"

"Not in such a case as this," I replied.

We rode on to the Maryland line, but could not overtake them. We were obliged to return, as it was near daybreak. The next day a friend of ours went to Maryland to see what had been done with Williams. He went to Dr. Savington's, and the Doctor told him that the fugitive could not live,— the kidnappers had broken his skull, and otherwise beaten him very badly; his ankle, too, was out of place. In consequence of his maimed condition, his mistress refused to pay the men anything for bringing him home. That was the last we ever heard of poor John Williams; but we learned afterwards why we failed to release him on the night he was taken. The kidnappers heard us coming, and went into the woods out of the way, until we had passed them.

Awhile before this occurrence, there lived in a town not far away from Christiana a colored man who was in the habit of decoying fugitives fresh from bondage to his house on various pretexts, and, by assuming to be their friend, got from them the name of their master, his residence, and other needed particulars. He would then communicate with the master about his slave, tell him at what time the man would be at his house, and when he came at the appointed hour, the poor refugee would fall into the merciless clutches of his owner. Many persons, mostly young people, had disappeared mysteriously from the country, from whom nothing could be heard. At last the betrayer's connection with these transactions was clearly traced; and it was decided to force him to quit his nefarious business.

He was too wary to allow himself to be easily

taken, and a resort was had to stratagem. I, with others, thought he deserved to be shot openly in his daughter's house, and was willing to take the consequences.

At last this man's outrages became so notorious that six of our most reliable men resolved to shoot him, if they had to burn him out to do it. After I had sworn the men in the usual form, we went to his barn, took two bundles of wheat-straw, and, fastening them under the eaves with wisps, applied a lighted match to each. We then took our stations a few rods off, with rifles ready and in good condition,—mine was a smooth-bore, with a heavy charge.

The house burned beautifully; and half an hour after it ignited the walls fell in, but no betrayer showed himself. Instead of leaving the house by the rear door, as we had expected, just before the roof fell in, he broke out the front way, rushed to his next neighbor's, and left his place without an effort to save it. We had built the fire in the rear, and looked for him there; but he ran in the opposite direction, not only as if his life was in danger, but as if the spirit of his evil deeds was after him.

CHAPTER 5

A Posse Sets Forth

DURING THE SUMMER OF 1851 A CRISIS WAS ALSO brewing on Edward Gorsuch's farm, just south of Monkton, Maryland, above Baltimore on the York Road and less than fifty miles from Christiana as the crow flies.

Gorsuch was a Maryland farmer of English descent, an active member of the Southern Methodist Church, and politically a Whig. In 1851 he was fifty-six years old, the father of five children, and married to his second wife. His contemporaries described him as a courtly southern gentleman, a good citizen, and a good master to his slaves.

From his uncle, John Gorsuch, Edward had inherited about two hundred acres of good land and perhaps two dozen slaves, with the provision that each be made free when he reached the age of twenty-eight. Whether from duty or conviction, Gorsuch determined to follow the provisions of his uncle's will. When Jarett Wallace, a slave on the farm, became twenty-eight in 1849, Gorsuch set him free. He then offered him a job as his market man, hauling produce from the farm to sell in Baltimore. When Wallace accepted, his former master set about building him a tenant house.

It seemed to Gorsuch that the other younger slaves on the farm ought to be content, since they had their freedom to look forward to. But just after Wallace was freed, Gorsuch became aware of a growing restlessness among four of them. Noah Buley and Joshua Hammond were in their middle twenties and were only a few years away from freedom. Nelson Ford and George Hammond had six or seven years left to wait.

Nelson Ford was a small man, not very strong, and inclined to ill health. Gorsuch took care of him when he was ill and spared him the heavy work. Usually Nelson drove a team of workhorses, but if he was not feeling well, he was given a helper. Allowances such as these made Edward Gorsuch consider himself a kindly and reasonable master.

In the fall of 1849 trouble began in earnest on the Gorsuch farm. A considerable amount of the wheat crop, which had been stored in the corn house between the mansion and barn, seemed to be missing. Gorsuch usually ground his own wheat in his own mill, and sold the flour in Baltimore. He could not account for the shortages.

Nearby, a Quaker named Elias Mathews ran a mill. Edward Gorsuch inquired of Mathews whether he had been asked to grind any extra wheat lately. Mathews told him that a free black man, Abraham Johnson, had been bringing considerable quantities of wheat to be ground. Since Johnson had neither land to raise wheat nor credit with which to buy it, it seemed a bit peculiar to Mathews. Nevertheless, he had asked no questions and had ground the wheat.

Gorsuch was angry. He did not like Quakers much anyway, and it seemed to him that Mathews had been irresponsible. Gorsuch was sure it was his own wheat that Johnson had stolen, taken to be ground, and sold as flour.

Gorsuch determined to get a warrant for Johnson's arrest on the charge of theft. He asked the local sheriff to serve the warrant, but the man was too slow and too good-natured to get to it. Gorsuch then gave the job to a local vigilante, Bill Foster, who was a terror to the blacks in that part of Maryland. Upon hearing that Foster was on his tail, Johnson hurriedly left the area and settled in Pennsylvania. Gorsuch applied to the governor of Pennsylvania for Johnson's extradition, but since no crime had been proved against the black, the extradition request was not honored.

Meanwhile Gorsuch suspected that his own slaves had helped Johnson steal the wheat. He began to question them closely, and possibly to threaten them with Bill Foster if they did not tell the truth. The four younger slaves grew restless; they had many hurried conversations.

It was November by this time, and the farmhands were busy cutting and topping the corn, and bringing the unshucked ears to the barn by oxcart. Almost every night the whole household got together for a merry corn-husking bee. Watching the singing and the dancing with an indulgent eye, Edward Gorsuch likely concluded, as many slave owners had before him, that the simple blacks were happy and contented in his care.

One dark night, however, there was no corn husking. The next morning Edward's son, Dickinson Gorsuch, aroused the whole household with the news that "the boys are all gone."

During the night the four slaves had slipped out of a skylight in their quarters behind the cornhouse, and had driven the big wagon to Baltimore. Sending the wagon back to Gorsuch, they had then taken the train to Philadelphia, and from there a local branch line to Penningtonville. Shortly thereafter they all settled down as farmhands in the vicinity of Christiana, using various aliases to prevent detection, and remained there for almost two years, until the events of the Christiana riot.

Gorsuch was enraged. That his kind treatment should be repaid in this fashion seemed to him monstrously unfair. The four slaves after all were his property, and should remain so until he set them free. He certainly could not afford to replace them. He felt he had been robbed of that property by Abraham Johnson, along with the wheat, and he began to suspect that the abolitionists of nearby Lancaster County, whom he had despised all his life, were somehow behind the whole affair.

The more he thought about it, the more sure he became that his own "boys" would never have betrayed him without the prodding of outside agitators. Several months after the slaves ran away, he received a message from them, he claimed, asking him to send food and clothing to a certain depot. It is hard to know whether this really happened or not. Having been treated as dependent children all their lives, the runaways may have seen nothing strange in asking for such help after they left their master. At any rate Gorsuch began to feel sure that they were practically being held against their will by the northerners. All the years of Maryland-Pennsylvania border animosity fed his anger. He became a man with one fixed idea: to get his slaves back from Pennsylvania.

Edward's son Dickinson tried to dissuade him. The slaves were gone. Of the four, two would have been free shortly anyway and one was sickly. The fourth was scarcely worth all the effort. Let bygones be bygones. But Edward would not be persuaded. His sense of justice was outraged.

On the same night as Edward Gorsuch's slaves fled, his nephew, Dr. Thomas Pearce, also lost a slave. Other neighbors, the Hutchings and the Nelsons, had had slaves disappear. As the months went by Gorsuch began to talk more and more seriously about getting a party together to go to Pennsylvania to look for the whole bunch.

Almost a year after the escape of his four slaves, the passage of the Fugitive Slave Law in September of 1850 encouraged Edward Gorsuch. He and those he recruited anticipated no difficulty in recovering their slaves, once located, since federal law and federal marshals would be on their side. For Gorsuch and his friends and relatives it was a good law. If obeyed, it would make possible the continuation of the Union. It was their positive duty to test it.

One year later, on September 1, 1851, Gorsuch

learned the exact whereabouts of his slaves. Padgett, the clock mender and informer of Sadsbury Township, sent him a letter:

Lancaster Co 28 August, 1851

Respected friend, I have the required
Information of four men that is within
Two miles of each other. now the best
Way is for you to come as A hunter
Disguised about two days ahead of your son and
let him come
   By way of Philadelphia and get the deputy mar-
   shal John
   Nagle I think is his name. tell him the situation
And he can get force of the right kind it will take
   them
About twelve so that they can divide and take them
All within half an hour. now if you can come on
   the 2nd or 3d of September come on & I will
Meet you at the gap when you get their
Inquire for Benjamin Clay's tavern let
Your son and the marshal get out
Kinyer's hotel now if you cannot come
At the time spoken of write very soon
And let me know when you can
I wish you to come as soon as you possibly can
very respectfully thy friend
                William M. P.
                William Padgett

Gorsuch decided to act on Padgett's advice, although he did not follow Padgett's timetable. Instead (according to Dickinson Gorsuch's diary), he set out for Philadelphia almost a week later on September 8, taking the express train. There he applied to Edward D. Ingraham, the United States commissioner, for four warrants directed to Henry H. Kline, deputy United States marshal, to arrest the fugitives. Why he was assigned to Kline, a deputized Philadelphia police officer, instead of Nagle, as Padgett suggested, is not clear.

The next day, September 9, Dickinson Gorsuch, his cousin Joshua Gorsuch, Dr. Thomas Pearce, and two neighbors, Nicholas Hutchings and Nathan Nelson, who had also lost slaves, went to Philadelphia by train. The following day they took the "cars" (the commuter line) to Parkesburg, a small town a few miles east of Christiana, where they joined up with Edward Gorsuch.

Gorsuch had hired two constables, John Agin and Thomas Tully, to help in arresting the escaped slaves. With these two men, Kline, and the six Marylanders there would be nine in the arresting party. This was not the force of twelve that Padgett had recommended, but Edward Gorsuch apparently was convinced that his "boys" wanted to come home and would go with him as soon as they saw him. In fact, according to one story handed down in the Gorsuch family, Edward Gorsuch claimed that he had received a message from the boys asking him to come and get them. In light of what finally happened at Christiana such a message seems unlikely. The story does reveal that Gorsuch saw himself as a kind and fatherly master, and not as an avenging tyrant, when he came to Lancaster County.

As it turned out there were not even nine in the arresting party. Henry Kline was supposed to meet the others in Parkesburg on Wednesday, the tenth. However, in order to throw abolitionist spies off his trail he came by a different route, taking a wagon to Penningtonville, a small village near Parkesburg and Christiana. From Penningtonville he intended to go back to Parkesburg, thus fooling any who were suspicious of his destination.

His plan, however, did not work. His wagon broke down before he reached Penningtonville, and when he arrived in that hamlet about midnight and stopped at the tavern for a drink, he was recognized by a black man named Samuel Williams, an agent of the Philadelphia Vigilance Committee. Kline had been drinking all day and was at least half drunk. Alarmed by the sight of Williams, he tried to throw him off the track by saying in a loud voice to the tavern keeper that he had come to look for some horse thieves.

"Your horse thieves have been here and gone—I understand all about your business," Samuel Williams remarked. "You'll have to be a little quicker next time."

Instead of spending the night in Penningtonville, Kline decided to go on to Gap, hoping to mislead Williams. In Gap he stopped at several taverns, asked loudly about horse thieves, and had more to drink. Finally he slept for a few hours, then hurried to Edward Gorsuch and his party in Parkesburg.

"But where are the constables? Where are Agin and Tully," Gorsuch wanted to know after Kline had told his confused story. Kline said that the two had come to Parkesburg the day before, and having somehow missed connections with the Gorsuch party had returned to Philadelphia to spend the day. They would be back on the night train. Accordingly the party met the midnight train from Philadelphia at Downingtown. But though they went through all the cars twice, they found no trace of the two constables.

Gorsuch was determined to proceed anyway. He had been in contact with Padgett and had set up a rendezvous for early the next morning. He was sure that everything would turn out all right, even though there were only seven of them to bring back his four slaves.

Just after midnight, therefore, on September 11, they all took a train from Downingtown to Gap. Arriving at Gap about 1:30 A.M. they got off and walked down the railroad tracks for a couple of miles to the place where Padgett had said he would meet them. Heavily muffled and wearing a mask, the informer silently came forward at their arrival. Motioning to them to follow, he led them down back roads and through cornfields to the Valley Road, which ran east to Christiana.

It was still dark, and the valley shrouded in a dense fog when, after four or five miles of hiking, they came to the entrance of the long lane that passed William Parker's house as it ran south across the valley to the Noble Road. Realizing that they were about to reach their destination, they walked even more quietly than before.

Suddenly a swift stream cut across their path. Padgett, who was in the lead, gave the signal to stop. He whispered to Gorsuch, then turned and started back the way he had brought them.

"Padgett says our boys are in a house owned by a nigger named Parker," Gorsuch whispered to the others. "He says they don't know we are coming but that we ought to be careful. It's just a bit down the road here. This is a good place to rest and see to our ammunition."

One man passed around cheese and crackers from his carpetbag, and the party squatted by the creek and ate a meager breakfast as they checked their guns. It was now about four o'clock in the morning and the sky was still heavy with night. As they finished their meal and began to stretch their legs, a sleepy cock crowed.

CHAPTER 6

———— ·◆· ————

Before the Battle

THE HOUSE TOWARD WHICH THE MARYLAND PARTY was creeping in the early hours of the morning was a small stone tenant house on the farm of Levi and Sarah Pownall, a Quaker family. For the past two years William Parker, his wife Eliza, and their three small children had lived there, sharing the house with another family: Eliza's sister, Hannah Pinckney, her husband, Alexander Pinckney (Parker's constant companion in his adventures), and their children.

The Pownall farm was set in a wide valley that stretched westward from the hamlet of Christiana all the way into Bart Township. On a ridge to the north ran Valley Road, and along the southern ridge, Noble Road. Near the center of the valley flowed a small swift stream, Valley Run. The long lane ran from north to south, connecting Valley Road to Noble Road and crossing the stream. It was at this crossing that the Gorsuch party breakfasted after Padgett had left them.

The Parker house lay about five hundred feet south

of the stream, where the ground began to rise toward the wooded south ridge. The house itself was set back from the long lane, but connected to it by a short lane. Behind the house was a shed, a good-sized barn, and a garden. Between the house and the stream grew a large orchard. All was neatly enclosed by a rail fence. The local people spoke of the fence as "the bars."

It was a relatively isolated location. The nearest house was occupied by Castner Hanway, about a mile west on Noble Road. Hanway had recently come into the area to operate a small grain mill on Valley Run. Neither an abolitionist nor a Quaker, Hanway lived alone with his wife, Martha, and kept to himself. People in the area knew him as a peaked-looking man around thirty, always dusted with flour from his mill.

Besides the Hanways' place, there were in the vicinity the big house of the Pownall farm, about two fields over, the farm of Joseph Scarlett, off the long lane to the north, and a log cabin occupied by George Steele about a half mile away.

Despite the lack of neighbors close by, the Parkers and the Pinckneys had no chance to be lonely. Ever since they had moved to the Pownall farm, the little stone tenant house had been used as a gathering place for the local blacks. They came to wash their clothes in the nearby stream, to husk corn and make apple butter, to talk over their growing problems and fears.

Among those who frequented the Parker house were the escaped slaves of Edward Gorsuch, all living and working on various farms nearby. Although they were using assumed names, and although it was almost two years since their escape, they lived in constant fear of recapture and looked to Parker as their protector.

During the days just preceding the arrival of the Gorsuch party, there had been much coming and going at the Parker house. Samuel Williams, the advance man for the Philadelphia Vigilance Committee, had come into the neighborhood—although not to Parker's—and had left a report that Gorsuch was coming for his slaves. Joseph Scarlett, Parker's neighbor, had returned from a business trip to Philadelphia with the same piece of news.

With so much advance warning it would have been possible to slip the Gorsuch slaves out of the country before the Maryland party arrived. It might even have been prudent for William Parker to leave. He was not a Gorsuch slave, but the Gap gang was so determined to get rid of him that they would probably try to involve him in the next mass pickup of escaped slaves.

Instead, Parker chose to stand and fight. The northern resistance to the new Fugitive Slave Law, the stories in the antislavery press about heroic rescues, the frustration he had felt in the John Williams affair, all strengthened his resolve. He had strong support from local abolitionists. Few in the immediate neighborhood had attended the meeting in the Bart Township schoolhouse, where the group pledged itself not to obey the new law, but most approved of that pledge.

The Gorsuch party offered Parker a chance to make a clear-cut stand against the legitimacy not only of the new law but of slavery itself. Previously he had attacked slave agents and slave kidnappers, but here was a legitimate slave owner coming after his escaped slaves. If Parker and his band were now strong enough to defy his authority, it might mean the end, once and for all, of such forays into this part of Pennsylvania at least. All that he had accomplished in the past years were but prelude to this one act of defiance.

Parker decided not only to stay and fight, but to protect the Gorsuch slaves by keeping them temporarily at his house. This must have quickly become known throughout the area. Otherwise, Padgett would not have led the Gorsuch party to Parker's house, but would have taken them instead to the various farms where the slaves ordinarily lived and worked.

Parker's employers, the Pownalls, also heard that the escaped slaves were staying with Parker and that an incident was likely. One night Sarah Pownall, a matronly woman of about fifty, walked across the fields to have a talk with Parker. By chance it turned out to be the very night before the riot.

"If these rumors are true, and the slave owners do come, I wish thee would consider whether it would not be better to escape to Canada rather than lead the colored people to resistance by force of arms," she told him.

"If the laws protected us colored men as they do white men, I would be a nonresistant and not fight, but appeal to the laws," Parker told her. "But the laws for personal protection are not made for us, and we are not bound to obey them. If a fight occurs, I want the whites to stay away. They have a country and may obey the laws. But we have no country."

Unhappy, but unable to persuade him, Sarah returned home. The Parkers and Pinckneys meanwhile began to prepare for a party later that evening. Perhaps to keep the morale of the community high and ready for self-defense, Parker had invited the local blacks to join his household in making a pot of apple butter from the windfalls in the nearby orchard.

The apple butter boiled in a huge caldron over an open fire in the front yard. While it simmered and spat, the group danced around it, then quieted and sang a mournful song:

> *"The bloodhound's baying at my back*
> *The master's just behind*
> *Lest he's resolved to take me back*
> *Before I cross the line*
> *O Lijah's father, why not pity me*
> *And lead me on to Canada*
> *Where colored men are free."*

The party broke up early since work on the local farms started at dawn. In addition to the Pinckney and Parker families three black men spent the night in the little stone tenant house. They were Abraham Johnson (not the same man as stole the Gorsuch wheat), Samuel Thompson, and Joshua Kite. The latter two were Gorsuch's slaves, Joshua Hammond and Nelson Ford, as they were known under their new names. A third Gorsuch slave, Noah Buley, came back the next morning to take part in the fight. The fourth presumably slipped away.

All five men were armed with guns or clubs, and Eliza and Hannah with corn cutters. Not knowing when or where the southerners would strike, the household settled down to an uneasy night's sleep.

CHAPTER 7

The Riot

IT WAS JUST A LITTLE BEFORE 5:00 A.M. AND DAWN was beginning to break when the Gorsuch party left their resting place by the side of the stream and started up the long lane toward William Parker's house. Off to the right they heard a horn blowing. It might have been the summons for farmhands or railroad workers to come to breakfast; or it might have been a signal. No one was ever quite sure.

Edward Gorsuch and Henry Kline were in the lead. Just as they reached the short lane leading to Parker's house, they saw the figure of a man coming toward them. In the dimness of the early morning it was hard to tell much about him at first, but as they came closer to one another Edward Gorsuch gasped. The man looked very much like his slave Nelson Ford. In the same instance he saw the figure of another man and thought he recognized Joshua Hammond. For their part the two men gave a great shout of warning, and ran back toward the house.

The entire Maryland party gave chase, hoping to

catch them before they reached the safety of shelter. Thomas Pearce and Dickinson Gorsuch, who were bringing up the rear, jumped the rail fence and took a shortcut through the orchard. The two black men, however, reached the house ahead of their pursuers, and ran right upstairs to the second floor, leaving the front door open.

In hot pursuit Gorsuch and Kline raced through the open door and found the downstairs empty. Everyone was on the second floor.

"I am the deputy United States marshal," Kline shouted up the stairs. "I have warrants here for the arrest of Nelson Ford and Joshua Hammond."

"No one here with those names," someone shouted back from upstairs.

Kline and Gorsuch started upstairs, but on the landing were met with a vicious looking five-pronged fishgig. Then an ax came hurtling down at them, and they retreated hastily to the foot of the stairs. Here Kline attempted to read the full warrants to the occupants, barely able to make out the words in the faint light.

"I don't care about you or your warrant," the voice above called down.

"Come on, Mr. Gorsuch, we better try talking to them from outside," Kline suggested.

The two stepped outside. Immediately someone threw a board out of the window, which hit Thomas Pearce and gave him a black eye; another object struck Joshua Gorsuch on the shoulder. Then one of the blacks fired twice, and a bullet passed through Edward Gorsuch's hat. Kline aimed his gun toward the window from which the shot had come and fired back, but no one was hit.

After this initial burst of gunfire a battle of words began. Kline kept stating his authority as deputy United States marshal, and kept reading his warrants. After a time a handsome light-skinned black man appeared at the upstairs window. It was William Parker. Parker reiterated that there was no one in the house by the names cited on the warrants.

"You may know them by different names," Joshua Gorsuch suggested. The Marylanders up to this point seemed to believe that the blacks would give up once they understood that the full force of federal law was against them.

Edward Gorsuch then declared that he had a right to his property. Parker said he did not believe that one man had the right to own another. Gorsuch quoted the Scriptures to prove that slavery was acceptable. Parker quoted it back to prove that it was not. Dickinson Gorsuch was amazed to hear any black man quote the Bible so readily as Parker had.

It was a scene unique in history. The Maryland party, heavily armed, stood about in the chilly dawn before a humble tenant house, while the middle-aged, respectable slave owner below argued about the merits of slavery itself with the handsome young slave above him. Behind Parker, the figures of other blacks kept moving back and forth. There were only four other men, two women, and several children on the second floor of the tenant house, but Kline began to fear that there were many more. He decided it was not going to be quite as easy as he had thought to take them by force. Consequently, he determined to frighten them into submission.

Handing a note to Joshua Gorsuch, he commanded him in a loud voice to go to the nearest town and come back with a force of a hundred men. Joshua pretended to go; actually, he hid nearby.

The Parker party, too, thought it needed reinforcements. After consulting with William, Eliza Parker decided to blow the horn that was used within the black community as a signal that emergency help was needed. When she began blowing it from an upstairs window, two members of the Gorsuch party climbed a peach tree that grew near the house and fired at her. They missed completely, and Eliza merely ducked down beneath the windowsill and kept on blowing.

In answer, small groups of local blacks began to assemble from all directions armed with scythes, guns, corn cutters, and stones. To the frightened Gorsuch party it seemed as though over a hundred came swiftly in response to the call. Probably there were only thirty to forty assembled. Likewise Parker and his party imagined that a large number of whites came to reinforce the Marylanders, though in fact, only a few white neighbors arrived on the scene, mainly after the fighting was over. One of the new black arrivals was another Gorsuch slave, Noah Buley. He was riding a handsome gray horse and carrying a gun.

The blowing of the horn stirred up the whole valley. Several miles from Parker's house a local storekeeper, Elijah Lewis, was just beginning his day when Isaiah Clarkson, a free black, came rushing up, all out of breath. Clarkson was an elderly man, highly respected in the community. Lewis was disposed to listen attentively to what he had to say.

"Parker's is surrounded by kidnappers," Clarkson told Lewis excitedly. "They have broken in and are about to take Parker away. Will you go down there and see that justice is done?"

Lewis was a Quaker and an abolitionist. Until now he had taken no active part in the underground railroad or in the rescue of kidnapped slaves, but he shared with some of his neighbors a resolve not to obey the Fugitive Slave Law and to resist kidnappings. When he heard Clarkson say kidnappers were at Parker's, he did not hesitate but started out immediately on foot to see what was going on.

On his way down Noble Road, Lewis passed the lane entrance to the house of the newly arrived miller, Castner Hanway. Lewis did not know exactly what Hanway's sentiments would be in this case, but thinking that two men might be better than one, he stopped and asked the miller to go with him. Hanway, as we have seen, was neither a Quaker nor an abolitionist, but he evidently felt it was his duty to see that there was no illegal disturbance in the neighborhood. He was not feeling well that morning, so he decided to ride his sorrel mare. Entering the long lane from the south, while Lewis cut across the fields on foot, Hanway was unwittingly the first white neighbor to arrive at Parker's house.

The blacks in the besieged house cheered the arrival of all reinforcements, including Hanway. There were now perhaps thirty or forty blacks standing in the fields across from the house. The Gorsuch party began to feel outnumbered and distinctly uneasy.

For a while, apparently, the Marylanders did not notice Hanway in the crowd, although several of them later testified in court that they heard the blacks cheer when he rode up. Joshua Gorsuch was the first to observe that there was a white man sitting quietly on his horse at the end of the short lane. It was easy to jump to the conclusion that he had responded to the same signal as the rest, and was, in fact, their leader. Gorsuch pointed Hanway out to Kline. Kline then went over to him, told him that he was the United States marshal, and handed him the warrant to read. When Lewis arrived a few minutes later (according to Parker's account, Lewis was the first to arrive), Kline gave the warrant to him too. Lewis did not have his glasses, but he could make out that it was a legal document.

Kline then requested that they help him.

Hanway shook his head. "The colored people have a right to defend themselves," he insisted. Then looking over the crowd of armed blacks he added, "You had better leave or there will be bloodshed. You need not come here to make arrests, for you can't do it."

Kline realized that this was true and was suddenly frightened. He told Hanway and Lewis that he was holding them responsible for the Gorsuch slaves. Exactly what he meant is not clear. Evidently he intended to retreat, then at a more propitious time return to the area and demand of Hanway and Lewis that they produce the runaways. At any rate he shouted to the Gorsuch party, who stood near the Parker house, to withdraw, and then, as if to set an example, bolted over the fence and into the cornfields.

Lewis and Hanway too were alarmed by the look of things. They had originally gone to Parker's to prevent a kidnapping. When they discovered the United States marshal was present to make some arrests, they refused to cooperate with him, thus defying the new Fugitive Slave Law. Now they saw no other role for themselves in an increasingly dangerous situation. Their sympathies were with the blacks, but the blacks were armed and in the majority. As nonresisters, they could not help in the coming struggle. They decided instead to withdraw. Lewis went south up the long lane to the Noble Road, and Hanway turned his horse north toward the stream. Despite sounds of battle behind them, they did not turn back.

Deserted by the marshal, and also frightened by the look of the black crowd, the small group of six southerners began to withdraw in an orderly fashion down the long lane. Parker and his small band of followers had come outside by this time and were standing in the short lane arguing with the Marylanders up to the last minute. As his party was leaving, a look of determination suddenly came over Edward Gorsuch's face and he turned around.

"I won't leave without my slaves. I'll have my property or go to hell," he shouted.

Gorsuch's sudden expression of rage seemed to

unleash the last restraints of Parker and his men, and they surged toward him. At the same time the new arrivals from the fields and the long lane began to close in. Dickinson Gorsuch, seeing his father's sudden peril, began to make his way toward him. Thomas Pearce attempted to shoot, but his gun would not go off. He then decided it would be prudent to flee. Joshua Gorsuch, Nathan Nelson, and Nicholas Hutchings also ran for their lives, leaving the two Gorsuches alone in the short lane to face the angry blacks.

A fierce battle now broke out. Afterward, no one was sure who fired first or who struck whom. Parker's account, written fifteen years later, records that Dickinson Gorsuch fired at him without wounding him, that Alexander Pinckney fired at Dickinson and hit him, and that Samuel Thompson (Joshua Hammond), Gorsuch's slave, was the first to attack Gorsuch.

Dickinson Gorsuch testified at the trial that after he saw Hanway reading the warrant he returned to the house and saw the blacks come out. Among them he recognized two former Gorsuch slaves.

They came shouting around me and one of them [Josh Hammond] said, "there he is, take him." I raised my revolver, and told them if they touched me I would shoot them. I told my father we had better go, for they intended to murder the whole of us. He said it would not do to give it up that way. We were at the house. I then walked nearer the bars [the rail fence]. While I was there, one of the men passed me [probably Lewis]. It was soon after this I saw them strike my father. They struck him with clubs. I went to him, as near as I could get, and put up my revolver to shoot them. I was struck across the right arm with a club, and about the same time I was shot in the side.

Edward Gorsuch fought bravely, despite his fifty-six years, but he was knocked to the ground, then shot, then hacked to death with a corn cutter. No one ever was sure who did it. Dickinson and Joshua Gorsuch thought it was probably one of his own slaves. Parker believed it was one of the women.

All these events—from the arrival of local blacks and Hanway and Lewis, to the flight of Marshal Kline and most of the southerners, to the wounding of Dickinson and the killing of Edward Gorsuch—were over in a few minutes. Later it was claimed that Hanway and Lewis's presence had encouraged the blacks and led to the final acts of violence. In any case the two had barely turned away when Edward Gorsuch was shot.

Bedlam followed the brief burst of fighting. Dickinson Gorsuch managed to stagger toward the end of the short lane. Here he was met by Kline who, having overcome his first fright, had returned from the cornfield. Kline led the wounded man a way further, left him under a tree, and went to seek help.

Joshua Gorsuch and Thomas Pearce ran down the long lane, pursued by a band of angry blacks. Joshua was struck several times on the head with a club, and Dr. Pearce was shot in his wrist and shoulder. They staggered on, afraid for their lives, and managed to catch up with Hanway just as he reached the stream. Joshua reached him first and implored the miller to take him up on his horse. Pearce was content to hang onto the stirrups and gasp for breath. Only Hanway and his horse stood between Pearce and his pursuers.

Hanway turned in the saddle and said to the blacks: "For the love of God boys, don't shoot." The mob paused uncertainly, then fell back, and began to turn away. Thomas Pearce told several people the next day that he thought he owed his life to the miller. Later at the trial he claimed Hanway was only trying to save his own skin.

Once the pursuers had turned away, Hanway, still feeling ill, and now frightened, left the men where they were and rode on up the stream toward his mill. Joshua Gorsuch and Thomas Pearce ran on toward the Valley Road, somehow getting separated in their flight.

While the members of Gorsuch's party were making good their escapes, a few neighbors began to arrive at the scene of battle. The first was Joseph Scarlett, the Quaker farmer who lived at the north end of the long lane and who had warned Parker of the coming of the Gorsuch party. Scarlett had been two and a half miles away when he heard that there was trouble at Parker's. He galloped the whole way back and arrived with his horse in a lather, just after the battle. The first thing he saw was Dickinson Gorsuch, lying under a tree in the long lane, coughing up blood. He immediately went to the southerner's aid, holding his head and giving him water to drink. Many believed Scarlett's actions saved Dickinson's life.

Another neighbor who arrived on the scene was Miller Knott. Earlier Knott's small son had heard the horn and seen men running and had crossed the fields to see what was happening at Parker's to cause all the excitement. Knott was a conservative, and no abolitionist, but he was worried about his son and came to see if he could find him.

At about the same time as Miller Knott, Isaiah Clarkson arrived, having made his slow way by foot across the fields since summoning Elijah Lewis. The blacks were still swarming around the Parker house in great numbers and in an angry mood. The sight of the killing of one slave master and the wounding of another had awakened a volcano of bitter memories and feelings within many of them, urging them on to further violence. Both Knott and Clarkson were frightened about what might happen. Clarkson got up on a stump in a cornfield and called the mob to order. He had to call three times, but eventually they heard him and gathered around. He told them that there had been enough bloodshed and that they had better disperse now, for they were in grave danger. The killing of a white man by black men was an unthinkable crime in those days. The whites would be sure to take swift and bitter vengeance.

The blacks listened to him; sobered, they left quietly in twos and threes.

Still another neighbor arrived. It was Lewis Cooper, Elijah Lewis's son-in-law, and he brought his Dearborn wagon. Levi Pownall, fetched by William Parker, came hurrying across the fields to help Dickinson. Pownall and Cooper decided to transport the wounded young man to the Pownalls' in the wagon, and then to use it to take the corpse of Edward Gorsuch to Christiana to await a coroner's inquest.

The riot had started at 5:00 A.M. with the arrival of the Gorsuch party. By 7:00 A.M. it was over, and by eight o'clock in the morning no one was left at the little stone tenant house. Inside sat a fresh tub of apple butter, uneaten. Outside the crows were greeting the beginnings of a fine September morning.

Some people called it the first battle of the Civil War. It had been fought between two small groups of men, white and black, each representing the issues at stake in the nation. Now it was over and a dreadful day of reckoning lay in store for the people of the neighborhood.

CHAPTER 8

PARKER'S ACCOUNT
The Riot

A SHORT TIME AFTER THE EVENTS NARRATED IN the preceding number, it was whispered about that the slaveholders intended to make an attack on my house; but, as I had often been threatened, I gave the report little attention. About the same time, however, two letters were found thrown carelessly about, as if to attract notice. These letters stated that kidnappers would be at my house on a certain night, and warned me to be on my guard. Still I did not let the matter trouble me. But it was no idle rumor. The bloodhounds were upon my track.

I was not at this time aware that in the city of Philadelphia there was a band of devoted, determined men,—few in number, but strong in purpose,—who were fully resolved to leave no means untried to thwart the barbarous and inhuman monsters who crawled in the gloom of midnight, like the ferocious tiger, and, stealthily springing on their unsuspecting victims, seized, bound, and hurled them into the ever open jaws of Slavery.

Under the pretext of enforcing the Fugitive Slave Law, the slaveholders did not hesitate to violate all other laws made for the good government and protection of society, and converted the old State of Pennsylvania, so long the hope of the fleeing bondman, wearied and heartbroken, into a common hunting-ground for their human prey. But this little band of true patriots in Philadelphia united for the purpose of standing between the pursuer and the pursued, the kidnapper and his victim, and, regardless of all personal considerations, were ever on the alert, ready to sound the alarm to save their fellows from a fate far more to be dreaded than death. In this they had frequently succeeded, and many times had turned the hunter home bootless of his prey. They began their operations at the passage of the Fugitive Slave Law, and had thoroughly examined all matters connected with it, and were perfectly cognizant of the plans adopted to carry out its provisions in Pennsylvania, and, through a correspondence with reliable persons in various sections of the South, were enabled to know these hunters of men, their agents, spies, tools, and betrayers. They knew who performed this work in Richmond, Alexandria, Washington, Baltimore, Wilmington, Philadelphia, Lancaster, and Harrisburg, those principal depots of villany, where organized bands prowled about at all times, ready to entrap the unwary fugitive.

They also discovered that this nefarious business was conducted mainly through one channel; for, spite of man's inclination to vice and crime, there are but few men, thank God, so low in the scale of humanity as to be willing to degrade themselves by doing the dirty work of four-legged bloodhounds. Yet such men, actuated by the love of gold and their own base and brutal natures, were found ready for the work. These fellows consorted with constables, police-officers, aldermen, and even with learned members of the legal profession, who disgraced their respectable calling by low, contemptible arts, and were willing to clasp hands with the lowest ruffian in order to pocket the reward that was the price of blood. Every facility was offered these bad men; and whether it was night or day, it was only necessary to whisper in a certain circle that a negro was to be caught, and horses and wagons, men and officers, spies and betrayers, were ready, at the shortest notice, armed and equipped, and eager for the chase.

Thus matters stood in Philadelphia on the 9th of September, 1851, when Mr. Gorsuch and his gang of Maryland kidnappers arrived there. Their presence was soon known to the little band of true men who were called "The Special Secret Committee." They had agents faithful and true as steel; and through these agents the whereabouts and business of Gorsuch and his minions were soon discovered. They were noticed in close converse with a certain member of the Philadelphia bar, who had lost the little reputation he ever had by continual dabbling in negro-catching, as well as by association with and support of the notorious Henry H. Kline, a professional kidnapper of the basest stamp. Having determined as to the character and object of these Marylanders, there remained to ascertain the spot selected for their deadly spring; and this required no small degree of shrewdness, resolution, and tact.

Some one's liberty was imperilled; the hunters were abroad; the time was short, and the risk imminent. The little band bent themselves to the task they were pledged to perform with zeal and devotion; and success attended their efforts. They knew that one false step would jeopardize their own liberty, and very likely their lives, and utterly destroy every prospect of carrying out their objects. They knew, too, that they were matched against the most desperate, daring, and brutal men in the kidnappers' ranks,—men who, to obtain the proffered reward, would rush willingly into any enterprise, regardless alike of its character or its consequences. That this was the deepest, the most thoroughly organized and best-planned project for man-catching that had been concocted since the infamous Fugitive Slave Law had gone into operation, they also knew; and consequently this nest of hornets was approached with great care. But by walking directly into their camp, watching their plans as they were developed, and secretly testing every inch of ground on which they trod, they discovered enough to counterplot these plotters, and to spring upon them a mine which shook the whole country, and put an end to man-stealing in Pennsylvania forever.

The trusty agent of this Special Committee, Mr. Samuel Williams, of Philadelphia,—a man true and faithful to his race, and courageous in the highest degree,—came to Christiana, travelling most of the way in company with the very men whom Gorsuch had employed to drag into slavery four as good men as ever trod the earth. These Philadelphia roughs, with their Maryland associates, little dreamed that the man who sat by their side carried with him their inglorious defeat, and the death-warrant of at least one of their party. Williams listened to their conversation, and marked well their faces, and, being fully satisfied by their awkward movements that they were heavily armed, managed to slip out of the cars at the village of Downington unobserved, and proceeded to Penningtonville, where he encountered Kline, who had started several hours in advance of the others. Kline was terribly frightened, as he knew Williams, and felt that his presence was an omen of ill to his base designs. He spoke of horse thieves; but Williams replied,—"I know the kind of horse thieves you are after. They are all gone; and you had better not go after them."

Kline immediately jumped into his wagon, and rode away, whilst Williams crossed the country, and arrived at Christiana in advance of him.

The manner in which information of Gorsuch's designs was obtained will probably ever remain a secret; and I doubt if any one outside of the little band who so masterly managed the affair knows anything of it. This was wise; and I would to God other friends had acted thus. Mr. Williams' trip to Christiana, and the many incidents connected therewith, will be found in the account of his trial; for he was subsequently arrested and thrown into the cold cells of a loathsome jail for this good act of simple Christian duty; but, resolute to the last, he publicly stated that he had been to Christiana, and, to use his own words, "I done it, and will do it again." Brave man, receive my thanks!

Parker's
Account

Of the Special Committee I can only say that they proved themselves men; and through the darkest hours of the trials that followed, they were found faithful to their trust, never for one moment deserting those who were compelled to suffer. Many, many innocent men residing in the vicinity of Christiana, the ground where the first battle was fought for liberty in Pennsylvania, were seized, torn from their families, and, like Williams, thrown into prison for long, weary months, to be tried for their lives. By them this Committee stood, giving them every consolation and comfort, furnishing them with clothes, and attending to their wants, giving money to themselves and families, and procuring for them the best legal counsel. This I know, and much more of which it is not wise, even now, to speak: 't is enough to say they were friends when and where it cost something to be friends, and true brothers where brothers were needed.

After this lengthy digression, I will return, and

speak of the riot and the events immediately preceding it.

The information brought by Mr. Williams spread through the vicinity like a fire in the prairies; and when I went home from my work in the evening, I found Pinckney (whom I should have said before was my brother-in-law), Abraham Johnson, Samuel Thompson, and Joshua Kite at my house, all of them excited about the rumor. I laughed at them, and said it was all talk. This was the 10th of September, 1851. They stopped for the night with us, and we went to bed as usual. Before daylight, Joshua Kite rose, and started for his home. Directly, he ran back to the house, burst open the door, crying, "O William! kidnappers! kidnappers!"

He said that, when he was just beyond the yard, two men crossed before him, as if to stop him, and others came up on either side. As he said this, they had reached the door. Joshua ran up stairs, (we slept up stairs,) and they followed him; but I met them at the landing, and asked, "Who are you?"

The leader, Kline, replied, "I am the United States Marshal."

I then told him to take another step, and I would break his neck.

He again said, "I am the United States Marshal."

I told him I did not care for him nor the United States. At that he turned and went down stairs.

Pinckney said, as he turned to go down,—

"Where is the use in fighting: They will take us."

Kline heard him, and said, "Yes, give up, for we can and will take you anyhow."

I told them all not to be afraid, nor to give up to any slaveholder, but to fight until death.

Parker's
Account

"Yes," said Kline, "I have heard many a negro talk as big as you, and then have taken him; and I'll take you."

"You have not taken me yet," I replied; "and if you undertake it you will have your name recorded in history for this day's work.

Mr. Gorsuch then spoke, and said,—"Come, Mr. Kline, let's go up stairs and take them. We *can* take them. Come, follow me. I'll go up and get my property. What's in the way? The law is in my favor, and the people are in my favor.

At that he began to ascend the stair; but I said to him,—"See here, old man, you can come up, but you can't go down again. Once up here, you are mine."

Kline then said,—"Stop, Mr. Gorsuch. I will read the warrant, and then, I think, they will give up."

He then read the warrant, and said,—"Now, you see, we are commanded to take you, dead or alive; so you may as well give up at once."

"Go up, Mr. Kline," then said Gorsuch, "you are the Marshal."

Kline started, and when a little way up said, "I am coming."

I said, "Well, come on."

But he was too cowardly to show his face. He

went down again and said,—"You had better give up without any more fuss, for we are bound to take you anyhow. I told you before that I was the United States Marshal, yet you will not give up. I'll not trouble the slaves. I will take you and make you pay for all."

"Well," I answered, "take me and make me pay for all. I'll pay for all."

Mr. Gorsuch then said, "You have my property."

To which I replied,—"Go in the room down there, and see if there is anything there belonging to you. There are beds and a bureau, chairs, and other things. Then go out to the barn; there you will find a cow and some hogs. See if any of them are yours."

He said,—"They are not mine; I want my men. They are here, and I am bound to have them."

Thus we parleyed for a time, all because of the pusillanimity of the Marshal, when he, at last, said,—"I am tired waiting on you; I see you are not going to give up. Go to the barn and fetch some straw," said he to one of his men. "I will set the house on fire, and burn them up."

"Burn us up and welcome," said I. "None but a coward would say the like. You can burn us, but you can't take us; before I give up, you will see my ashes scattered on the earth."

By this time day had begun to dawn; and then my wife came to me and asked if she should blow the horn, to bring friends to our assistance. I assented, and she went to the garret for the purpose.

When the horn sounded from the garret window, one of the ruffians asked the others what it meant; and Kline said to me, "What do you mean by blowing that horn?"

Parker's Account I did not answer. It was a custom with us, when a horn was blown at an unusual hour, to proceed to the spot promptly to see what was the matter. Kline ordered his men to shoot any one they saw blowing the horn. There was a peach-tree at that end of the house. Up it two of the men climbed; and when my wife went a second time to the window, they fired as soon as they heard the blast, but missed their aim. My wife then went down on her knees, and, drawing her head and body below the range of the window, the horn resting on the sill, blew blast after blast, while the shots poured thick and fast around her. They must have fired ten or twelve times. The house was of stone, and the windows were deep, which alone preserved her life.

They were evidently disconcerted by the blowing of the horn. Gorsuch said again, "I want my property, and I will have it."

"Old man," said I, "you look as if you belonged to some persuasion."

"Never mind," he answered, "what persuasion I belong to; I want my property."

While I was leaning out of the window, Kline fired a pistol at me, but the shot went too high; the ball broke the glass just above my head. I was talking to Gorsuch at the time. I seized a gun and aimed it at Gorsuch's breast, for he evidently had instigated Kline to fire; but Pinckney caught my arm and said, "Don't shoot." The gun went off, just grazing Gorsuch's shoulder. Another conversation then ensued between Gorsuch, Kline, and myself, when another one of the party fired at me, but missed. Dickinson Gorsuch, I then saw, was preparing to shoot; and I told him if he missed, I would show him where shooting first came from.

I asked them to consider what they would have done, had they been in our position. "I know you want to kill us," I said, "for you have shot at us time and again. We have only fired twice, although we have guns and ammunition, and could kill you all if we would, but we do not want to shed blood."

"If you do not shoot any more," then said Kline, "I will stop my men from firing."

They then ceased for a time. This was about sunrise.

Mr. Gorsuch now said,—"Give up, and let me have my property. Hear what the Marshal says; the Marshal is your friend. He advises you to give up without more fuss, for my property I will have."

I denied that I had his property, when he replied, "You have my men."

"Am I your man?" I asked.

"No."

I then called Pinckney forward.

"Is that your man?"

"No."

Abraham Johnson I called next, but Gorsuch said he was not his man.

The only plan left was to call both Pinckney and Johnson again; for had I called the others, he would have recognized them, for they were his slaves.

Abraham Johnson said, "Does such a shrivelled up old slaveholder as you own such a nice, genteel young man as I am?"

At this Gorsuch took offence, and charged me with dictating his language. I then told him there were but five of us, which he denied, and still insisted that I had his property. One of the party then attacked the Abolitionists, affirming that, although they declared there could not be property in man, the Bible was conclusive authority in favor of property in human flesh.

"Yes," said Gorsuch, "does not the Bible say, 'Servants, obey your masters'?"

I said that it did, but the same Bible said, "Give unto your servants that which is just and equal."

At this stage of the proceedings, we went into a mutual Scripture inquiry, and bandied views in the manner of garrulous old wives.

When I spoke of duty to servants, Gorsuch said, "Do you know that?"

"Where," I asked, "do you see it in Scripture, that a man should traffic in his brother's blood?"

"Do you call a nigger my brother?" said Gorsuch.

"Yes," said I.

"William," said Samuel Thompson, "he has been a class-leader."

When Gorsuch heard that, he hung his head, but said nothing. We then all joined in singing,—

> *"Leader, what do you say*
> *About the judgment day?*
> *I will die on the field of battle,*
> *Die on the field of battle,*
> *With glory in my soul."*

Then we all began to shout, singing meantime, and shouted for a long while. Gorsuch, who was standing head bowed, said, "What are you doing now?"

Samuel Thompson replied, "Preaching a sinner's funeral sermon."

"You had better give up, and come down."

I then said to Gorsuch,—" 'If a brother see a sword coming, and he warn not his brother, then the brother's blood is required at his hands; but if the brother see the sword coming, and warn his brother, and his brother flee not, then his brother's blood is required at his own hand.' I see the sword coming, and, old man, I warn you to flee; if you flee not, your blood be upon your own hand."

It was now about seven o'clock.

"You had better give up," said old Mr. Gorsuch, after another while, "and come down, for I have come a long way this morning, and want my breakfast; for my property I will have, or I'll breakfast in hell. I will go up and get it."

He then started up stairs, and came far enough

to see us all plainly. We were just about to fire upon him, when Dickinson Gorsuch, who was standing on the old oven, before the door, and could see into the up-stairs room through the window, jumped down and caught his father, saying,— "O father, do come down! do come down! They have guns, swords, and all kinds of weapons! They'll kill you! Do come down!"

The old man turned and left. When down with him, young Gorsuch could scarce draw breath, and the father looked more like a dead than a living man, so frightened were they at their supposed danger. The old man stood some time without saying anything; at last he said, as if soliloquizing, "I want my property, and I will have it."

Kline broke forth, "If you don't give up by fair means, you will have to by foul."

I told him we would not surrender on any conditions.

Young Gorsuch then said,—"Don't ask them to give up,—*make* them do it. We have money, and can call men to take them. What is it that money won't buy?"

Then said Kline,—"I am getting tired waiting on you; I see you are not going to give up."

He then wrote a note and handed it to Joshua Gorsuch, saying at the same time,—"Take it, and bring a hundred men from Lancaster."

As he started, I said,—"See here! When you go to Lancaster, don't bring a hundred men,—bring five hundred. It will take all the men in Lancaster to change our purpose or take us alive."

He stopped to confer with Kline, when Pinckney said, "We had better give up."

"You are getting afraid," said I.

"Yes," said Kline, "give up like men. The rest would give up if it were not for you."

"I am not afraid," said Pinckney; "but where is the sense of fighting against so many men, and only five of us?"

The whites, at this time, were coming from all quarters, and Kline was enrolling them as fast as they came. Their numbers alarmed Pinckney, and I told him to go and sit down; but he said, "No, I will go down stairs."

I told him, if he attempted it, I should be compelled to blow out his brains. "Don't believe that any living man can take you," I said. "Don't give up to any slaveholder."

To Abraham Johnson, who was near me, I then turned. He declared he was not afraid. "I will fight till I die," he said.

At this time, Hannah, Pinckney's wife, had become impatient of our persistent course; and my wife, who brought me her message urging us to surrender, seized a corn-cutter, and declared she would cut off the head of the first one who should attempt to give up.

Another one of Gorsuch's slaves was coming along the highroad at this time, and I beckoned to him to go around. Pinckney saw him, and soon became more inspirited. Elijah Lewis, a Quaker, also came along about this time; I beckoned to him, likewise; but he came straight on, and was met by Kline, who ordered him to assist him. Lewis asked for his authority, and Kline handed him the warrant. While Lewis was reading, Castner Hanway came up, and Lewis handed the warrant to him. Lewis asked Kline what Parker said.

Kline replied, "He won't give up."

Then Lewis and Hanway both said to the Marshal,—"If Parker says they will not give up, you had better let them alone, for he will kill some of you. We are not going to risk our lives";—and they turned to go away.

While they were talking, I came down and stood in the doorway, my men following behind.

Old Mr. Gorsuch said, when I appeared, "They'll come out, and get away!" and he came back to the gate.

I then said to him,—"You said you could and would take us. Now you have the chance."

They were a cowardly-looking set of men.

Mr. Gorsuch said, "You can't come out here."

"Why?" said I. "This is my place. I pay rent for it. I'll let you see if I can't come out."

"I don't care if you do pay rent for it," said he. "If you come out, I will give you the contents of these";—presenting, at the same time, two revolvers, one in each hand.

I said, "Old man, if you don't go away, I will break your neck."

I then walked up to where he stood, his arms

resting on the gate, trembling as if afflicted with palsy, and laid my hand on his shoulder, saying, "I have seen pistols before to-day."

Kline now came running up, and entreated Gorsuch to come away.

"No," said the latter, "I will have my property, or go to hell."

"What do you intend to do?" said Kline to me.

"I intend to fight," said I. "I intend to try your strength."

"If you will withdraw your men," he replied, "I will withdraw mine."

I told him it was too late. "You would not withdraw when you had the chance,—you shall not now."

Kline then went back to Hanway and Lewis. Gorsuch made a signal to his men, and they all fell into line. I followed his example as well as I could; but as we were not more than ten paces apart, it was difficult to do so. At this time we numbered but ten, while there were between thirty and forty of the white men.

While I was talking to Gorsuch, his son said, "Father, will you take all this from a nigger?"

I answered him by saying that I respected old age; but that, if he would repeat that, I should knock his teeth down his throat. At this he fired upon me, and I ran up to him and knocked the pistol out of his hand, when he let the other one fall and ran in the field.

My brother-in-law, who was standing near, then

· 105 ·

said, "I can stop him";—and with his double-barrel gun he fired.

Young Gorsuch fell, but rose and ran on again. Pinckney fired a second time, and again Gorsuch fell, but was soon up again, and, running into the cornfield, lay down in the fence corner.

I returned to my men, and found Samuel Thompson [Joshua Hammond] talking to old Mr. Gorsuch, his master. They were both angry.

"Old man, you had better go home to Maryland," said Samuel.

"You had better give up, and come home with me," said the old man.

Thompson took Pinckney's gun from him, struck Gorsuch, and brought him to his knees. Gorsuch rose and signalled to his men. Thompson then knocked him down again, and he again rose. At this time all the white men opened fire, and we rushed upon them; when they turned, threw down their guns, and ran away. We, being closely engaged, clubbed our rifles. We were too closely pressed to fire, but we found a good deal could be done with empty guns.

Old Mr. Gorsuch was the bravest of his party; he held on to his pistols until the last, while all the others threw away their weapons. I saw as many as three at a time fighting with him. Sometimes he was on his knees, then on his back, and again his feet would be where his head should be. He was a fine soldier and a brave man. Whenever he saw the least opportunity, he would take aim. While in close quarters with the whites, we could load and fire but two or three times. Our guns got bent and out of order. So damaged did they become, that we could shoot with but two or three of them. Samuel Thompson bent his gun on old Mr. Gorsuch so badly, that it was of no use to us.

When the white men ran, they scattered. I ran after Nathan Nelson, but could not catch him. I never saw a man run faster. Returning, I saw Joshua Gorsuch coming, and Pinckney behind him. I reminded him that he would like "to take hold of a nigger," told him that now was his "chance," and struck him a blow on the side of the head, which stopped him. Pinckney came up behind, and gave him a blow which brought him to the ground; as the others passed, they gave him a kick or jumped upon him, until the blood oozed out at his ears.

Nicholas Hutchings, and Nathan Nelson of Baltimore County, Maryland, could outrun any men I ever saw. They and Kline were not brave, like the Gorsuches. Could our men have got them, they would have been satisfied.

One of our men ran after Dr. Pierce [Pearce], as he richly deserved attention; but Pierce caught up with Castner Hanway, who rode between the fugitive and the Doctor, to shield him and some others. Hanway was told to get out of the way, or he would forfeit his life; he went aside quickly, and the man fired at the Marylander, but missed him,—he was too far off. I do not know whether he was wounded or not; but I do know, that, if it had not been for Hanway, he would have been killed.

Having driven the slavocrats off in every direction, our party now turned towards their several homes. Some of us, however, went back to my house, where we found several of the neighbors.

The scene at the house beggars description. Old Mr. Gorsuch was lying in the yard in a pool of blood, and confusion reigned both inside and outside of the house.

Levi Pownell [Pownall] said to me, "The weather is so hot and the flies are so bad, will you give me a sheet to put over the corpse?"

In reply, I gave him permission to get anything he needed from the house.

"Dickinson Gorsuch is lying in the fence-corner, and I believe he is dying. Give me something for him to drink," said Pownell, who seemed to be acting the part of the Good Samaritan.

When he returned from ministering to Dickinson, he told me he could not live.

The riot, so called, was now entirely ended. The elder Gorsuch was dead; his son and nephew were both wounded, and I have reason to believe others were,—how many, it would be difficult to say. Of our party, only two were wounded. One received a ball in his hand, near the wrist; but it only entered the skin, and he pushed it out with his thumb. Another received a ball in the fleshy part of his thigh, which had to be extracted; but neither of them were sick or crippled by the wounds. When young Gorsuch fired at me in the early part of the battle, both balls passed through my hat, cutting off my hair close to the skin, but they drew no blood. The marks were not more than an inch apart.

A story was afterwards circulated that Mr. Gorsuch shot his own slave, and in retaliation his slave shot him; but it was without foundation. His slave struck him the first and second blows; then three or four sprang upon him, and, when he became helpless, left him to pursue others. *The women put an end to him.* His slaves, so far from meeting death at his hands, are all still living.

CHAPTER 9

Parker's Escape

B Y 9:00 A.M., THE MORNING OF THE RIOT, THE POW-nall family had put the wounded Dickinson Gorsuch to bed in their front parlor and had sent for the local doctor. When the young southerner was conscious they explained to him carefully that they had "no unity with his cruel business" of slave catching, but as Quakers they were bound to care for him as a precious human being.

In fact, Dickinson Gorsuch remained with the Pownalls for over three weeks. He even fell slightly in love with a daughter of the family, Elizabeth Pownall. Although he returned to Maryland, married, and spent the rest of his life as a Maryland farmer, he never forgot the kindness of the Quaker family.

During the first day of his stay, Dickinson was considered dangerously ill, and members of the Pownall family tiptoed in and out. Gradually, as news of the morning's events spread, people began to assemble around the big farmhouse. There were curious and concerned neighbors as well as United States commissioners, deputy marshals, newspaper reporters, and police officers.

One by one the remaining members of the Gorsuch family turned up, each with a tale to tell. Marshal Kline appeared, still badly frightened, and told a rambling story of his efforts to find a doctor for Dickinson. It was clear to those who listened to him that he was mainly trying to get as far as possible from the scene of violence.

Nicholas Hutchings and Nathan Nelson next arrived and claimed that they had left the Parker house because they had been ordered by Kline to trail Elijah Lewis and Noah Buley, respectively, but listeners noted that they had run some distance from the area before they had stopped at a local farmhouse to ask for breakfast.

Thomas Pearce was reluctant to speak about his adventures, and went immediately to the side of the wounded Dickinson, whom he began to treat.

The last to show up was Joshua Gorsuch, who did not arrive until night. The blow Gorsuch had received on the side of his head had made him "crazy as a bedbug," and he had spent most of the day traveling about the area on wagons and passenger trains without knowing where he was or what he was doing. Coming to his senses at last in Columbia, he decided to return to Christiana.

In the course of the afternoon the local police decided to place a cordon around the Pownall farmhouse. They were influenced by Kline, who seemed to believe that the violence at Parker's was the beginning of a black uprising, and who feared that the blacks might attack the farmhouse wherein lay the wounded man.

Sarah Pownall, with the calm strength for which she was well known, set to work to feed all these visitors, welcome and unwelcome. Her daughters, Eleanor and Elizabeth, were kept busy all afternoon baking bread and pies and fetching milk and butter from the springhouse.

Meanwhile, Levi Pownall, Jr., the twenty-four-year-old son of the family, was having a series of adventures. In the morning, when Lewis Cooper brought Dickinson Gorsuch to the Pownall house in his Dearborn, Levi had looked out and seen William Parker and Alexander Pinckney standing near one of the farm sheds. Parker had come to be sure Dickinson was cared for. Levi hurried out and urged the two to hide. "You are in great danger," he told them. "Better plan to leave for Canada as soon as it's dark."

Later in the afternoon, when the excitement at the big house seemed to have died down a little, Levi went down to the Parker house to see if he could pack some clothes for the two. George, his younger brother, went with him. They found not only clothes, but Parker and Pinckney's loaded guns. This meant, Levi reasoned, that in the final battle they were unarmed. They, therefore, could not have been the ones to shoot Edward Gorsuch.

He searched the house a bit more, and was surprised to find a number of letters hidden behind a loose board. He took them back to the big farmhouse and read them, discovering that they were addressed to

Parker by a number of slaves he had helped to escape. The letters mentioned aid given by others also. Levi thought that since Parker could not read, the letters must have been read to him by local sympathizers. In addition, he felt sure that if the letters fell into the hands of federal marshals, they would implicate several local families, as well as lead to the detection of some refugees still in the United States. He decided to burn them all.

After dark, Parker and Pinckney approached the farmhouse, evidently unaware that it was heavily guarded. One of the Pownall daughters saw them from the kitchen window and hurried outside to lead them into the house before they were seen. She brought them through a door left temporarily unwatched and hurried them into a dark room. In the hallway they passed so close to a police officer that the girl's skirts brushed against him.

With the help of Sarah it was decided to dress Parker and Pinckney in Quaker gray suits and wide-brimmed hats and let them walk out the front door, each with a lady on his arm, thus slipping away under the very eyes of those looking for them.

While the girls went through their father's and brother's closets for the proper clothes, Sarah filled a pillowcase with food for the journey and asked her six-teen-year-old son George to put it under a certain tree at some distance from the house. When George returned, she told Parker exactly where to find the food. The gift was most welcome, for the men had not eaten all day.

Now all was in readiness for Parker and Pinckney's exit. With admirable self-possession the two Pownall daughters chattered away to their two escorts as they walked across the porch, down the steps, and out onto the grass.

George Steele, a local ironmonger who at that time was courting Elizabeth, was at the house that night and watched the whole charade with great admiration. Later he married Elizabeth, and wrote about the Parker escape in his memoirs.

In spite of this lucky start, the Pownall family could hardly believe that Parker could get out of the country safely. As the days passed, and every newspaper in the country began to feature the events in Christiana and publish descriptions of William Parker, they feared more and more for his safety. He was wanted everywhere by the police for his part in the "foul murder." How could he slip unnoticed through the country?

Nevertheless, a few weeks later, the family came down to breakfast one morning to find a letter slipped under the door that stated that Parker was safe in Canada. They never knew who wrote the letter, nor where it came from, but they were greatly relieved by the news.

Dickinson Gorsuch, still a patient at the house, had meanwhile heard a rumor that Parker had been caught and killed. "I hope it isn't true," he said, "for he was a noble nigger." Dickinson always insisted that Parker did not kill his father, and, in fact, had tried to restrain the others from doing so. And he never forgot his admiration for the black man who quoted Scriptures so eloquently from the upstairs window.

CHAPTER 10

GEORGE STEELE'S ACCOUNT

In 1918 GEORGE STEELE, THE HUSBAND OF ELIZABETH Pownall, wrote his memoirs in the form of a short document: "Some Recollections of a Long and Unsuccessful Life." In it he describes the Christiana riot. Although he was writing sixty-seven years after the event, his memories of the circumstances concur with accounts written in the years immediately following the riot.

While I was living at Sadsbury Forges there occurred the Christiana Riot. I think it worthwhile to write down here a rather full account of my knowledge of that event.

At the time of the Christiana Riot, I was running the two Forges on the Octoraro, called the Sadsbury Forges, (which I had rented from the Sproul Estate) making charcoal iron. The Forges and the dams have disappeared long ago. The glen no longer echoes the noise of the Forge hammers and the Octoraro runs free and hears no sound save its own dashing. I was not at that time interested in the anti-slavery movement and I knew nothing of the underground railroad. But I had a number of colored men employed cutting wood, burning charcoal, driving teams, etc. I then lived in a small log house, less than half a mile from what was afterwards known as the Riot House. It was occupied by two colored families, Parkers and Pinckneys. They did not work for me. I knew Parker very well. He told me that when a slave, his owner was a sporting man and attended fairs and horse races and big sales and took him along and would arrange prize fights between him and some other man's slave, and bet money on him (Parker) and that he always won. Parker tired of this and ran away. His owner never sent for him. Undoubtedly the colored people of the neighborhood were determined to resist the enforcement of the Fugitive Slave Law and Parker was their leader. It is equally certain that some white men who had colored men employed, when it was known that slave catchers were at Parker's house, said to their men, go and take your gun.

On the day of the Riot (September 11, 1851) I had planned to go to Lancaster on business and to walk over to Christiana to take the cars. I heard the racket at Parker's house and determined to go that way and see what was the matter, but when I got as far as the Noble Road, I met some colored men that I knew and they told me what had happened, that one white man was killed and another of the slave holders badly wounded. They seemed very exultant. I told them they were in great danger and if anyone who had anything to do with it had any sense at all, they would leave the country before night.

I went to Lancaster and returned to Christiana as soon as I could. That evening and the next day the greatest excitement prevailed in the neighborhood. The commissioner who had the enforcement of the fugitive slave law in charge had his headquarters at Zercher's Hotel in Christiana and there were a great many (special constables, I suppose) from Philadelphia and from the neighborhood who were scouring the country around and bringing in colored men to have a hearing before the commissioner. The principal witness against them was a man named Kline, who was one of the party that went to Parker's house to capture the slaves. There was a colored man named Lew Christmas who drove team for me. Some time before, he told me that he was a free man and got me to write to a gentleman at Elkton who knew all about him. The Elkton man replied that Lew Christmas was a free man, that his father was Jerry Christmas, a free man who was a fiddler, and in demand at dance parties and for that reason was named Christmas. Lew's wife sewed this letter in a bag and Lew always carried it around his neck. Christmas and I were together at the mule stable a few minutes after the firing was heard and I knew he could not have been there, but he was arrested. I went before the Commissioner and Lew produced his letter and they let him go.

Anthony E. Roberts, a Lancaster County man, was U. S. Marshal for the district. He had been appointed by Zachary Taylor, who was then dead and succeeded by Millard Fillmore.

When the fighting was over at the Riot House, Steele's Account Parker hurried over to Pownall's to get a wagon to take the wounded man where he could be attended to. Parker and Levi Pownall, Jr., ran to get a horse and wagon, but before they geared up, a neighbor brought the wounded man over in a dearborn. Levi then told Parker and Pinckney that they were up against the government of the United States and that there was no safety for them in the country. They went away and concealed themselves somewhere until that night. Levi went over to the Riot House where he found a great number of letters relating to the escape of fugitive slaves to Canada. Some of these letters would have incriminated several persons for violating the fugitive slave law, so he burned them all. George Pownall (who was then a boy) found Parker's and Pinckney's guns. They were loaded and apparently had not been fired off. This would seem to confirm what had been said by someone—that Parker had gone out unarmed to persuade the slave owners to go away.

At night of the day of the riot, Dickinson Gorsuch—the wounded man—was not expected to live. There were a great many of his friends and neighbors in the Pownall House and the house was surrounded by a crowd, principally the special constables who had come up from Philadelphia.

· 119 ·

They appeared to be guarding the house. Some of them professed to fear that the colored people would attack the wounded man. Elizabeth Pownall, who afterwards became my wife, and her

sister, Ellen, were washing dishes in the kitchen when Parker and Pinckney walked in through the out kitchen door. They had been concealed all day and did not know what was going on. Fortunately, one of the Pownall girls had presence of mind enough to blow out the candles and open the stair door and motion to the two men to go upstairs. Mrs. Pownall, who was in the sitting room waiting on the wounded man, was sent for, and the family and one of the neighbors went into the pantry. For a few minutes the silence was dense. Then Mrs. Pownall (who was the best and most capable woman I ever knew) whispered to the girls, "Get a clean pillow case and fill it with bread and meat." There was a whispered remonstrance, "All these people in the house to feed and barely enough bread for breakfast." Mrs. Pownall whispered back, "Mix more bread." The pillow was filled. Levi Pownall, Jr., went upstairs and provided the men with clothes and hats. George Pownall took the pillow case of food out to the orchard and left it at the foot of the queen apple tree. At a favorable time the two colored men were brought down and charged not on any account to speak a word, and the two Miss Pownalls walked beside them to the gate. If the guards saw them, they supposed them to be callers on the young ladies. One morning when the Pownall family came down, they found a letter under the front door addressed to Elizabeth B. Pownall. It said Parker is safe in Canada. They never knew who wrote it or where it came from. The same day that they got this letter, Dickinson Gorsuch's brother visited him, and brought a newspaper which had an account of Parker's having been caught in New York State and cut to pieces. When he had read the account to his brother and gone out of the room, Dickinson called Elizabeth (who was in the room) to his bedside and said, "Miss Pownall, I watched your face while my brother was reading that newspaper, and from your expression I know you don't believe a word of it. I believe Parker is safe in Canada, and I am glad of it, for he was a noble nigger."

The history of the Christiana Riot can hardly be understood without knowing something about a gang of horse thieves and counterfeiters who had their headquarters at Clemson's Tavern near Mount Vernon. They had started the business of slave capturing. One of them named Padget was nominally a mender of clocks and tramped over the country and cultivated intimacy with run-away slaves and found out where they came from and the names of their owners and would write to the slave owners and guide them when they came to arrest their slaves, and get a reward. Gorsuch's slaves were not living at the Parker house. It is my opinion that Padget guided the Gorsuchs there for the purpose of running Parker into slavery, as he interfered with the business of the Clemson gang [evidently another name for the Gap gang]. But Gorsuch's slaves came to the Parker house armed with guns and they probably shot their owners.

Steele's
Account

CHAPTER 11

More Escapes

WHILE THE POWNALLS WERE HELPING PARKER AND Pinckney escape, the wives of the two men were having desperate adventures. Right after the riot Eliza and Hannah gathered up their children and took them to the home of their own mother, the children's grandmother, who was herself an escaped slave and lived nearby. They did not seem to realize that they were in danger, having participated in a riot that led to the death of a southern gentleman on northern soil. They stayed at their mother's until they were arrested that same afternoon.

The deputy who had them in custody, however, had a kind heart, for when Hannah tearfully begged to be allowed to go back to her mother's house for her baby, he let her do so. He drove both women back in a Dearborn wagon and stopped by the edge of a field near the house in question. "Now go and get the baby and be quick about it," he told them.

Eliza and Hannah crossed the field. Minutes passed but they did not return. Finally the deputy came after them and found both the house and the cradle empty. Urged on by the intrepid Eliza, all three women had taken the children and slipped out the back way to hide in the woods. By nightfall, however, Hannah and Eliza's mother insisted on returning to her cabin. There, a few days later, she was captured and returned to her southern master. Later, a rumor spread that she had said she wanted to be a slave again. Most people thought that she must have been forced to say such words.

When their mother left them, Eliza and Hannah started out in the dark on their own search for safety. They knew the area well, but in their fright they became confused and wandered about in a circle, never getting more than five miles from their home. Early in the morning they found themselves on a road near the eastern boundary of Sadsbury Township.

There was a farmhouse in the distance and Eliza asked a passerby "who lives there?"

"Joseph Fulton" was the answer.

Eliza thought she recognized the name from William's talk of local abolitionists. Consequently she considered it safe to approach the house. She told Hannah to stay behind and be ready to run at any moment. Then she tapped on the door.

Mary Ann Fulton, answering the knock, immediately saw that the two women needed help, and hurried them into the kitchen.

"Who are you and what can I do for you?" she asked.

Eliza, evidently trusting something in Mary Ann's

manner, told her their names and their plight. Mary Ann thought quickly. She could hide the women in the barn, but she knew their farm was likely to be searched inside and out. No, it would be safest to get them out of the country at once.

She gave the women food and drink, then ordering one of the hired hands to get out the wagon, she ran to the field where her brother Ambrose was cutting corn, and asked his permission to take their youngest and fastest horse.

"What for?" he asked suspiciously.

When she told him her plans he argued with her. The adventure was too dangerous. If she persisted in it, she could be sued under the Fugitive Slave Law, and all their property would have to be confiscated in order to pay the fines. He would not let her have the horse.

Mary Ann felt her father would settle the matter in her favor, but he was not expected until evening. So she continued to argue with her brother until he grudgingly said that instead she might have their oldest and slowest horse, old blind Nance. Ambrose Fulton believed that with such a poor horse Mary Ann would never attempt the trip, but he underestimated her determination. She hitched up old Nance, provided the women with sunbonnets to shield their faces, and set forth without any clear idea of where she was going.

Mary Ann thought she remembered her father mentioning some abolitionist families around Caln meetinghouse in Chester County. She wasn't sure just where Caln was located, but she was determined to find it. Anything to get out of Lancaster County, which was beginning to buzz like an angry beehive in reaction to the riot.

Old Nance plodded along slowly, and Mary Ann did not dare hurry her for fear she would simply give out. The women sat silently beside her, absorbed in their own thoughts. Every once in a while they passed a suspicious-looking party on the road, but no one stopped them.

Reaching the Caln neighborhood in the late afternoon, she inquired discreetly at several farmhouses whether there were families in the area who would accept refugees, and everywhere she was refused. Word of the Christiana riot had appeared in the Philadelphia papers that morning, and people were frightened of becoming involved with anyone who might in any way be connected with the events of yesterday.

They drove into a little woods and there stopped to plan what to do. It was now dark, and Mary Ann had no idea how to proceed.

Just then, as if by luck, a small wrinkled black woman carrying a tub of laundry on her head came down the road toward them. Mary Ann hailed her, and began to explain their situation. "You need not tell me," the old woman said. "I knows, I knows all about it. I've helped in many a scrape like this. Just drive down the hill there, and you'll see my house. Just go in and set them down, and I'll be back in a little bit."

Mary Ann gratefully accepted her help. She left Eliza and Hannah in the cabin in the woods and made her way slowly back to Sadsbury, arriving home at dawn on Saturday morning, almost twenty-four hours after she set out. Old blind Nance had served her well.

According to the story of this adventure that has been handed down in the Fulton family, Eliza and Hannah made their way safely to Canada. According to court records, however, they were arrested a second time, perhaps in Chester County, but released on September 23. As a result of the newspaper accounts of the Christiana riot, Eliza's master was now on her trail. She had many dreadful experiences and had to leave her children behind in safe hands in order to escape him. Both women, nevertheless, eventually reached Canada and freedom.

CHAPTER 12

Terror in the Valley

O THER PARTICIPANTS IN THE CHRISTIANA RIOT ALSO made their escape with the help of local abolitionists. Shortly after the dispersal of those at the Parker house, Dr. Augustus Cain was interrupted in his morning practice by the arrival of his own farmhand, Henry C. Hopkins. Hopkins was holding his arm, saying he had been shot at Parker's. Cain removed the bullet from his forearm, but would not let Henry tell him anything about the affair. If questioned, he wanted to be able to say in truth that he knew nothing. Instead, he bandaged the wound, and told the man to get out of the county as soon as possible.

About an hour later another black man, John Long, came to the dispensary with a bullet in his thigh. This Dr. Cain extracted, again refusing to listen to the circumstances. Instead, he sent the man on his way with instructions to get out of the vicinity as quickly as he could.

At midnight of the same day three blacks who had taken part in the riot appeared at the home of Caleb

Hood, a prominent member of the underground railroad in Bart Township. Caleb advised them to hide in
the woods, since his house and barn would likely be
searched. He gave them some food and promised that
in the morning he would collect some clothes and some
wages due them from their employers.

The three had planned to leave for Canada the
next night, but when Caleb visited their families the
wife of one of the men sent an urgent message through
Caleb advising them not to go. Because the county was
being searched for participants in the Christiana riot,
every road out was closely guarded. She had a strong
and well-founded intuition that if they tried to escape
they would be captured.

Instead, the three men hid for two weeks until the
uproar died down. Instead of staying near Caleb
Hood's, they spent most of the time under the floor of
a small cabin belonging to a black family in Drumore
Township. At the end of two weeks Caleb took them to
the next station of the underground railroad and
started them on their long journey. They managed to
reach Canada safely.

The two blacks helped by Dr. Cain, the three
aided by Caleb Hood, Parker and Pinckney, their
wives, and the four Gorsuch slaves all made successful
escapes. All the other participants in the riot, and many
innocent people as well, were caught up in the dragnet
of eastern Lancaster County, which began to take shape
within hours after the events at Parker's.

Slowly at first, then with gathering speed, the legal

authorities began to deal with the crisis. The first step was a coroner's inquest. The county squire, Joseph Pownall, arranged for Edward Gorsuch's body to be brought to Fred Zercher's Hotel in Christiana and then summoned a coroner's jury.

United States Deputy Marshal Henry Kline had by this time reached Christiana and he testified at the inquest, assisted by several blacks he had managed to round up. One, Harvey Scott, was slightly feeble-minded and badly frightened. (Later he admitted that he had said everything Kline told him to say.)

The coroner's jury was composed of a good number of abolitionists, and their sentiments were revealed in the report they prepared after hearing the facts:

That on the morning of the 11th instant the neighborhood was thrown into an excitement by the above deceased, and some five or six persons in company with him, making an attack upon a family of colored persons, living in said township, near the Brick Mill, about 4 o'clock in the morning, for the purpose of arresting some fugitive slaves as they alleged, many of the colored people of the neighborhood collected, and there was considerable firing of guns and other fire-arms by both parties, upon the arrival of some of the neighbors at that place, after the riot subsided, found the above deceased, lying on his back or right side, dead. Upon post mortem examination upon the body of the deceased, made by Drs. Patterson and Martin, in our presence, we believe he came to his death by gunshot wounds that he received in the above mentioned riot, caused by some person or persons unknown.

In the course of the coroner's examination the note from Padgett with suggestions about how to capture his escaped slaves was found inside Gorsuch's hat. This news spread quickly through the valley and reached the little clockmaker. He thought it wise to slip away and was never again seen in that area.

Following the coroner's inquest the district attorney for Lancaster County, John L. Thompson, was notified that a murder had been committed. He hurried down from Lancaster to Christiana, arriving shortly after noon on Friday, and began to issue warrants for the arrest of suspects. Kline, who was the chief witness, did not know the names of the black people he had seen at the riot, but he was ably assisted by several informers and by members of the Gap gang. The outlaws were eager to help round up suspects. It was a perfect opportunity for them to get even with old enemies. They gave Kline the names of every black who might possibly have been at the riot, and many more besides. They also told him which abolitionists to have arrested, and which homes to order searched.

The local sheriff, William Proudfoot, could not personally arrest all those named. He quickly pressed into service a number of deputies, including many of the Irish immigrant workers then employed laying fresh track for the railroad near Christiana. As news of the riot spread, and roughs and rowdies from as far away as Philadelphia and Baltimore began to pour into

Christiana, he deputized them too.

Meanwhile Castner Hanway and Elijah Lewis, hearing that they were to be charged, came up to Christiana together to give themselves up. Henry Kline met them on the steps of Zercher's Hotel and confronted them angrily.

"You lily livered scoundrels," he said, "yesterday, when I pled for my life like a dog and begged you not to let the blacks fire upon us, you turned around and told them to do so."

Hanway did not answer, but Elijah Lewis denied the charge. Before the blacks started shooting, he reminded Kline, he and Hanway had left the scene, and Kline himself was off in the cornfields. Kline was so provoked by this rejoinder that he had to be restrained by Sheriff Proudfoot from attacking the two men.

By Friday afternoon it was clear to the district attorney, John Thompson, he would need still more men to make all the arrests Kline was demanding. He decided, therefore, to return to Lancaster Friday night and come back the next morning with a large party of armed men.

News of the events at Christiana had by this time reached the highest circles of government in Washington, along with a vehement demand for action from the state of Maryland. President Millard Fillmore and his secretary of state, Daniel Webster, immediately saw that the murder of Gorsuch would be seen by the whole South as proof that the federal government could not be counted on to enforce the new Fugitive Slave Law. Since the enforcement of this law was the crucial part of the Compromise of 1850 in the eyes of southerners, the whole compromise, so delicately put together, was in jeopardy.

It seemed necessary to act swiftly and decisively. The newspapers were printing highly distorted accounts of the riot, making it sound like a preplanned insurrection. Without waiting to ascertain whether this was true or not, the government decided that all the participants in the riot ought to be charged with treason against the United States on the grounds that they had conspired to make war on the United States government—embodied in the person of a duly appointed United States marshal.

Webster, in consultation with United States Attorney General John C. Crittenden, concluded that "even if a conviction were not obtained, the effect of the trial would be salutary in checking northern opposition to the enforcement of the Fugitive Slave Law."

John M. Ashmead, United States attorney for Pennsylvania, was informed of this decision, and ordered to proceed to Sadsbury Township with a suitable force to put down the "insurrection." Early Saturday morning, two days after the riot, he hurried out to Christiana accompanied by United States Marshal Anthony E. Roberts, forty-five United States marines, a detachment of Philadelphia police, and a civil posse of some fifty men!

Thompson, returning from Lancaster with his force, was extremely surprised to find these representatives of the federal government present. He was inclined at first to argue that since the crime had been committed on Lancaster County soil, the prisoners ought to be his. United States Commissioner Edward

Ingraham, the man who had issued the warrants for the arrest of the Gorsuch slaves, was also on the scene, and he ruled that under the new Fugitive Slave Law the crime was federal and that prisoners were prisoners of the United States government. Rather than sending Thompson and his men home, it was agreed that they could also make arrests and hold prisoners in the Lancaster County jail. All the prisoners, however, would be charged with treason against the United States government.

There were by now altogether over two hundred men ready to scour the countryside for suspicious characters. Among those deputized were members of the Gap gang, the Irish laborers (who had been taught to fear blacks as competition for their jobs), and the roughnecks recruited from Philadelphia and Lancaster. All the vigilantes were for one reason or another deeply antagonistic toward blacks and abolitionists, and their prejudices were enflamed by lurid articles appearing in the newspapers and by the widespread fear that the Christiana riot might somehow be the beginning of a black uprising.

A reign of terror ensued in the valley. Few of the special deputies cared anything about the niceties of the law, and even regular law enforcement officers went on a rampage. There was much drunkenness and some thievery. The homes of local abolitionists were turned upside down, women insulted and struck, horses stolen. Most of the blacks hid or fled. Those who were left were rounded up en masse.

For the conservatives of the area, who had been

opposed all along to the underground railroad, the murder of Gorsuch and the wounding of Dickinson was just the sort of tragedy they had expected to result from the activities of the meddlesome abolitionists. They were incensed that their liberal neighbors still did not see the light, but were treating the whole incident as though it were another kidnapping, even helping to hide the blacks. Nevertheless, these sentiments did not protect them. Their homes too were searched and their horses taken.

The seizure of the hired man of Thomas Whitson, an old and respected Quaker, typifies the attitudes of the special deputies making arrests. When Whitson saw what was happening, he followed the group down the road and asked them to release their victim. In reply, one of the men swore at him and flourished a revolver in his face, asking if he was not one of the abolitionists of the area.

"I am," said Thomas, "and I am not afraid of thy shooting me. So thee may as well put thy pistol down."

The deputy turned to the others, still swearing. "Shall I shoot him?" he asked.

"No, let the old Quaker go," they told him gruffly.

Peter Woods was a black teen-ager working on the farm of Joseph Scarlett, Parker's neighbor and sometime employer. His recollection of his arrest is vivid:

The day the fight happened I was up very early. We were to have "a kissing party" that night for Henry Roberts; and as I wanted to get off early I asked my boss, Joe Scarlett, if he would plough if I got up ahead and spread the manure. I started at it at two o'clock. The morning was foggy and dull. About daylight Elijah Lewis's son came running to me while I was getting my work done, and said that the kidnappers were here. I got there about seven or eight o'clock. I met some of them coming out of the lane, and others were on a run from the house. I met Hanway on a bald-faced sorrel horse coming down the long lane, and his party with him. The other party, the marshal and his people, took to the sprouts, licking out for all they could, and then took the Noble Road.

When Scarlett was arrested they were rough in arresting him. They took him by the throat, and pointed bayonets all around him. I said to myself if you arrest a white man like that, I wonder what you will do to a black boy? The arrests were made a day or two after the riot. I was plowing or working the ground and when I saw the officers come to make the arrests, I quickly unhitched and went toward Bushong's and soon there were six of us together and we went to Dr. Dingee's and hid. We heard a racket of horses coming and then we jumped into the graveyard. This was two days after the riot . . . Then they got us. The man with the mace, the marshal I guess, said "I got a warrant for Peter Woods." They pointed me out and then he struck me and then they tried to throw me. They arrested me and took me up a flight of stairs, and then they tied me. Then they started away with me and tried to get me over a fence. They had me tied around my legs and around my breast, and they put me in a buggy and took me to Christiana. From there they took me to Lancaster, and put me first in the old jail and then in the new prison.

There at Christiana was David Paul Brown and Thaddeus Stevens and Mr. Black. They had quarters in "old Harrar's store." We did not know who they were counsel for, and we thought they were threatening us, and trying to make us give ourselves away. Thad Stevens or someone said to me, "Who do you live with?" They had just brought me down from the Harrar garret. Mr. Brown then asked me again how I got up there in that garret, "Who put you there?" I made up my mind not to talk, and Brown said, "if you don't talk we will send you to jail."

Thaddeus Stevens, the famous abolitionist United States congressman from Pennsylvania referred to, and David Paul Brown, an abolitionist lawyer, had undertaken to represent the accused men and women. They worked many hours in Zercher's Hotel, interviewing those arrested, trying to sort out those who were participants in the riot from those who had no part in the riot but had been swept up in the dragnet.

In all, more than fifty of those arrested were held for further hearings. Those arrested by John Thompson were taken to Lancaster and held in the new jail, while those arrested by Ashmead were taken to Moyamensing, in the southern part of Philadelphia County. All were to be charged by the same grand jury.

George Steele, in his memoirs, describes the departure of the prisoners:

I cannot remember whether it was the day of the riot or the day after that Anthony E. Roberts, the U. S. Marshal, brought a company of marines up to Christiana. They stacked their muskets in front of Zercher's Hotel and stayed there until the prisoners were taken to Philadelphia. The scene at Christiana when the prisoners were taken to Philadelphia was one to be remembered. The prisoners were loaded in a car. The marines were getting on the train. Some Philadelphia politician, I forget his name, was addressing the crowd, protesting against the Marshal's removing the marines and declaring that the country was in a state of insurrection. No one seemed to be listening to him. The Clemson gang was very much in evidence. Two of them, Bill Blair and Perry Marsh, were drunk and quarreling and Clemson was trying to quiet them. Dan Caulsberry, one of the prisoners, was a forgeman who worked for me. I was talking to him at the car window about taking some care of his family while he was away and gave him a small amount of money that I owed him. Perry Marsh called out, "Look at Steele, he's giving them money." And he came running up to me and said, "If it had not been for the damned Abolitionists like you and yourself, these men would not have got in this trouble." I said to him, "Perry Marsh, sneak thief and jail bird, what do you want with me and myself?" Amos Clemson came waddling up and took Perry by the arm and led him away.

CHAPTER 13

The Ripples Spread

THE VIOLENCE THAT SPREAD THROUGH LANCASTER County after the Christiana riot gave expression to the deeply held fear of black insurrection prevalent throughout the country at this time. It was also an expression of anger against the abolitionists that had been building up for some time throughout the North. That anger had many sources: economic, political, and social.

Northern bankers and merchants feared that abolitionism would bring about secession. The harsh truth was that the South could get along better without the North than the North could without the South. The South could trade with England and survive, while secession would leave the North deprived of southern markets.

In order to offset the effects of abolitionist agitation, some northern businessmen encouraged antiabolitionist activity. By putting up posters and providing free beer, they promoted the formation of the huge mobs that collected in all the big northern cities to disrupt abolitionist meetings. The mobs were made up largely of white northern laborers whose fear of black competition for their jobs was further inflamed by pro-slavery propaganda.

Hatred of the abolitionists was thus reinforced by fear of the blacks. Those prejudices were deeply rooted and pervasive. Even those opposed to slavery somehow felt it was a more vicious crime for a black man to kill a white man than for a white man to kill a black man. Whites automatically assumed that they provided the leadership in any situation, even the underground railroad. It was this fact that kept some of the abolitionists from seeing that William Parker had played a heroic role in the defense of his brothers at Christiana.

People feared and hated the abolitionists because it was believed that their doctrines would lead to "amalgamation of the races," or intermarriage. Although many masters exploited slaves sexually, and many light-skinned blacks were born of these unions (including Parker himself), there was a strange double standard about sex in those days that made intermarriage taboo.

The abolitionists were also the radicals of their day. Only a handful believed in the overthrow of the state and the common use of all productive property; the majority held much more conservative economic views. As a group, however, they were widely regarded as being against everything, including God and motherhood.

Anger against the abolitionists, finally, drew upon the majority's opposition to the doctrine of civil disobedience. Americans in 1851 were probably much more accustomed to people refusing to obey unjust laws than we are today. The Quakers, who had played a prominent role in early America, had always refused to serve in the militia or pay war taxes. Henry David Thoreau had given a recent impetus to the idea when he spent a night in jail rather than pay his poll tax. The Garrisonians emphatically stated their opposition to obeying any law upholding slavery or supporting a state that tolerated slavery. Then, as much as now, however, people feared the effects of civil disobedience and thought the doctrine would lead to anarchy.

The abolitionists, in fact, had little to do with the Christiana riot. Probably white sentiment in his favor had influenced William Parker to make his stand, but to stand and fight was his decision alone. Sarah Pownall, as we have seen, tried to dissuade him. Castner Hanway, the first man on the scene, was only a concerned neighbor, not an abolitionist. Elijah Lewis was an abolitionist, but he hurried to the Parkers' to prevent another kidnapping, he thought, not to resist the Fugitive Slave Law. Joseph Scarlett, a more ardent abolitionist, was involved only in giving a warning of the approach of the Gorsuch party. He did not arrive at the riot scene until the fight was over. None of the three had attended the Bart Township meeting in protest against the Fugitive Slave Law.

These facts were entirely overlooked at the time, as the editorials in the Philadelphia newspapers in the days immediately following the riot make clear. The *Philadelphia Sun* wrote:

The unwarrantable outrages committed last week at Christiana, in Lancaster county, is a foul stain upon the fair name and fame of our state. We are pleased to see that officers of the federal and state governments are upon the tracks of those engaged in the riot and that several arrests have been made. We do not wish to see the poor misled blacks, who participated in the affair, suffer to any great extent—they were but tools. The men who are really chargeable with treason against the United States government and with the death of Mr. Gorsuch, an estimable citizen of Maryland, are unquestionably white, with hearts black enough to incite them to the commission of any crime equal in atrocity to that committed in Lancaster county. Pennsylvania has but one course to pursue—and that is to aid, and warmly aid, the United States in bringing to punishment every man engaged in the riot.

The *Philadelphia Bulletin* went even further:

The melancholy tragedy of Christiana in this state by which two citizens of Maryland lost their lives has established in blood the dangerous character of the modern abolitionists.

The fugitive slaves in question when they fired on the representatives of the law, only carried out in practice what the abolitionists constantly assert on principle—for years Garrison and his followers have been telling the Fugitives that they have a right to slay any man be he even master or public officer who attempts to impede their flight; and these deluded negroes by perpetuating the atrocities we record today, have only obeyed the advice of those they consider their best friends.

The *Washington Republic* also blamed the abolitionists but thought there were not enough Garrisonians in Lancaster County to account for the murder.

Along with the first account of the atrocity that we published yesterday morning was a report that it originated in consequence of some leading abolitionists advising the negroes to stand their ground, that is, to resist and to arm and fight. We are no friends or apologists of abolitionists but we must say we find it difficult to believe there can be any foundation for such a dreadful charge. Were it the bedlamites of more Northern regions—the Garrisons, the Abby Kelleys, the Frederick Douglasses who have made the name equally ridiculous and odious—were it the theatrical and atheistical crackbrains, who declare their independence alike of the laws of God and man, against whom the accusation was made, it would be credible enough, because they have continually preached such doctrines and been proud to be abused and laughed at on account of them. But we are not aware there are any such fanatics in Pennsylvania and we should never go looking for them in Lancaster county.

Only the abolitionist newspapers refused to join in the chorus. Garrison's *Liberator* had gone to press when the news came through, but there was room in the next issue for a short paragraph:

So much for slavery! So much for the accursed Fugitive Slave Law. They who are responsible for this bloody transaction are the upholder of that law and that foul system. Fillmore, Webster & Co. The blacks are fully justified in what they did, by the Declaration of Independence, and the teachings and example of Washington, Warren [a revolutionary hero] and Kossuth [a Polish hero].

The *New York Independent,* a newspaper with strong antislavery leanings, blamed it all on the Fugitive Slave Law:

The recent affray at Christiana is only a new phase of the Hydra that was begotten by the spirit of compromise. The framers of this law counted upon the utter degradation of the negro race—their want of manliness and heroism—to render feasible its execution. Had they been dealing with the Indian race, they would not have ventured such an experiment. But it was the cowardly negro—the worm and not the serpent—upon whom they set their foot. They anticipated no resistance from a race cowed down by centuries of oppression, and trained to servility. In this however they were mistaken. They are beginning to discover that men, however abject, who have feasted upon liberty, soon learn to prize it and are ready to defend it. This discovery fills the advocates of the law with horror; visions of murder and treason gather thick about their heads; the Union groans and totters toward its fall. Yet fearful as the lesson is, it may prove salutary, and even merciful.

In Lancaster County itself the papers were outraged. The *Examiner and Herald* called it "one of the most horrid murders ever perpetuated in this county or state." The *Intelligencer* described it under a heading that read "Particulars of the Horrible Negro Riot and Murder."

Political issues were mixed into the uproar. William F. Johnston, the governor, was up for reelection. He was a member of the Whig party, which had a conservative wing called the "Silver Grays," and more radical wing called "The Woolly Heads." The Woolly Heads were abolitionists and included Thaddeus Stevens. The Silver Grays were neutral or mildly proslavery, but they did not take a strong stand for fear of losing the radical vote.

Johnston was a Silver Gray. The Democrats, opposing the Whigs, were strong in the South and, in consequence, strongly proslavery. Their candidate for governor of Pennsylvania was Colonel William Bigler.

Since Pennsylvania held its elections early in October in those days, both candidates were already hard at work stumping the state when the Christiana riot occurred. William Johnston, in fact, happened to pass through the area on his way from Harrisburg to Philadelphia the very morning of the riot. He did not stop to investigate, although word of the murder was already widespread and many curious travelers got off at the Christiana station to see what the excitement was all about.

For this omission he was roundly criticized. A committee of prominent Philadelphia Democrats called a public indignation meeting at Independence Square and wrote the Whig governor an open letter demanding that he act to vindicate the honor of the Commonwealth. A Democratic newspaper called the riot "the legitimate fruit of the policies pursued by Governor Johnston and Thaddeus Stevens." The Reverend J. S. Gorsuch, son of Edward and brother of Dickinson, published an open letter in a newspaper criticizing Johnston for his earlier failure to honor the extradition proceedings for Abraham Johnson, the black who was accused of selling the Gorsuch wheat, and for his slowness in providing sufficient men to make the Christiana arrests. The Lancaster County officials, Gorsuch claimed, had been forced to collect "a posse of men from the iron works and the diggings along the railroad to enforce the processes of the law."

Governor Johnston defended himself. He pointed out that state law enforcement officials had arrested many suspects and that he was offering a thousand dollar reward for the arrest of the person guilty of the murder. He also pointed out to his Philadelphia critics that it was ridiculous to suggest that there was any rebellion involved.

"There is no insurrectionary movement in Lancaster county, and there would be no occasion to march a military force there, as you seem to desire, and inflame the public mind by any such strange exaggeration," he wrote a trifle tartly.

But people were frightened of insurrection, and the Democratic candidates played on their fears. In Columbia, a few days after the riot at a Democratic campaign meeting, the principal speaker denounced "the horrid murder to Gorsuch by a band of desperate negroes excited and influenced by murderous abolitionists whose reeking hands are still smoking with the warm life blood of a fellow human being."

In the midst of all this excitement a preliminary examination of the Christiana prisoners was held on Tuesday, September 23, in Lancaster, before Lancaster County Alderman J. Franklin Reigart. Henry Kline told his version of the riot story, insisting that Castner Hanway had urged or ordered the blacks to shoot. Dr. Thomas Pearce confirmed that both Lewis and Hanway had refused to assist the marshal. Miller Knott described his experience in coming upon the scene after Gorsuch was killed and finding the blacks in a state of murderous excitement. Harvey Scott, the slightly feebleminded witness at the coroner's inquest, now stated positively that he saw Henry (Simms), one of the black prisoners, shoot Edward Gorsuch and that he saw John Morgan, another black prisoner, cut and hack him with a corn cutter. Together these witnesses made a strong case for the charge that there had been a conspiracy ahead of time to attack the Gorsuch party, with Hanway and Lewis as its leaders.

At this preliminary hearing Thaddeus Stevens spoke on behalf of the accused. He pointed out that there were actually no substantial charges against Hanway and Lewis, who merely acted out of neighborly concern. He told the alderman about the effect of the recent kidnapping of the black man at the home of Marsh Chamberlain, and how his savage beating had upset the whole area. After this event, he stated, it was natural that people reacted strongly to the rumor that another kidnapping was taking place.

Stevens was eloquent, but he failed to convince the Lancaster County alderman that the men were innocent of wrongdoing. Most of the prisoners were remanded to Philadelphia to await a hearing before the grand jury on the charge of treason. A few of the men were let go free, and all of the women were discharged, a form of sexual discrimination that in this instance benefited them. Among those freed were Eliza Parker and Hannah Pinckney, who were able to start their long journey to Canada.

The same evidence, plus brief arguments by the lawyers on each side of the case, was heard later the same week by the grand jury. On September 29 the Honorable John K. Kane, United States district judge in Philadelphia, instructed the jury on the legal aspects of the case. He explained the provisions of the Constitution relating to the return of fugitive slaves and those relating to treason. Treason was making war against the United States, and could be defined as assembling a large armed group with the intent of making war—or defying federal laws.

In theory, the judge's instructions were supposed to be impartial. It was up to the grand jury to decide whether to indict the prisoners for treason, or for the lesser charge of refusal to obey the Fugitive Slave Law, or to return them to Lancaster County to await trial on various charges, murder, or participating in an armed riot. In fact, however, the judge was strongly committed to the enforcement of the Fugitive Slave Law and strongly opposed to the abolitionists. He evidently hoped very much that the trial would implicate such men as Garrison, and he allowed his bias to be apparent. He spoke of the meeting in Bart Township at which both residents and strangers had been present, and at which "exhortations were made and pledges were interchanged to hold the law of the recovery of fugitive slaves of no validity, and to defy its execution.

"The supremacy of the constitution, in all its provisions is at the very basis of our existence as a nation," he went on. "He, whose conscience or theories of political or individual right forbid him to support and maintain it in its fullest integrity, may relieve himself from the duties of citizenship by divesting himself of its rights."

In other words, conscientious objectors to slavery ought to leave the country.

He also exhorted the jurors that they did not have to limit themselves to citizens of Pennsylvania, and if they found that "men have been among us, who, under whatever mask of conscience or peace, have labored to incite others to treasonable violence, and who, after arranging the elements of mischief, have withdrawn themselves to await the explosion they have contrived," the jury must feel free to implicate these people too.

In other words, go after the Garrisonians.

On October 7, the grand jury brought indictments against forty-one persons for treason against the United States. Among them were Hanway, Lewis, and Scarlett as well as Peter Woods, Henry Simms (the man accused of shooting Gorsuch), Nelson Ford, Joshua Hammond, and William Parker. The latter three, of course, were not prisoners, having escaped the night of the riot.

The following day, October 8, was election day. Governor Johnston lost to the Democrat, Bigler, by a slim margin. Most observers thought it was a result of the Christiana riot.

The treason trial was scheduled for late in November. People awaited its commencement with great interest. There had been only a few such trials before in the history of the United States. The whisky insurrections of western Pennsylvania were the cause of a treason trial in 1795; and in 1799 John Fries was tried for treason after he encouraged many people to resist the tax collectors when they came to collect a house tax. In 1807 Aaron Burr was accused of scheming with others to create in northern Louisiana a nation separate from the United States and was tried for treason, although eventually acquitted. Four other treason trials were of only minor interest.

So lawyers pored over dusty volumes, newspaper editors sharpened their pens, and politicians made speeches. All eyes were on Philadelphia. Few people realized that the United States government had made the decision to try the forty-one persons for treason for political reasons. Everyone knew, however, that the outcome of the trial would have a powerful effect upon the future enforcement of the Fugitive Slave Law and thus upon the outcome of the continuing struggle between North and South. It might even put a permanent damper on the abolitionists and their belief that they could put their individual consciences above the law of the land.

CHAPTER 14

The Treason Trial

N0 ONE AWAITED THE COMING TREASON TRIAL MORE eagerly than the Christiana prisoners who were locked up in the Philadelphia County Jail at Moyamensing.

Moyamensing had been built in 1832 as a model of the new penitentiary, or separate confinement system of imprisonment. The idea, new at the time, was to place each prisoner in a separate cell and prevent him from communicating with his fellow prisoners in any way. The cells were approximately eight by twelve feet, and the prison, built to look like a medieval castle, was supposed to house three hundred prisoners in all. However, within a few years of its opening it was overcrowded, and two or more prisoners had to be placed in each cell. The building itself was cold and drafty, and though each cell had a fireplace, the prisoners were forbidden to use them.

As a result, several fell ill with colds and bronchitis. Castner Hanway was sick through November and December, and the judge ordered that he be removed from the cell he shared with Elijah Lewis and placed in a more comfortable apartment in the debtors' prison, where his wife could attend him. One prisoner had to be taken to the hospital, and several others shifted to warmer cells.

The black field hands or tenant farmers who had been gathered up hastily during the reign of terror in Lancaster County had only the thin work clothes they had brought with them. The Philadelphia Vigilance Committee, hearing of their plight, raised money to buy them warm clothes, and the women of the Female Anti-Slavery Society, under the leadership of the Quaker abolitionist Lucretia Mott, set about sewing clothes for the men.

To be locked in a cold dismal prison, either all alone or with only one cell mate, was a fearful experience for everyone. Some of the men were particularly frightened and used to pray so loudly that an audience gathered outside the prison walls to hear them. Dan Caulsberry, who worked for George Steele, is supposed to have prayed for Kline, who had given false witness against him: "Lord, catch Kline, shake him well, shake him over the fiery pit—but don't let him drop in."

The witnesses whom the prosecution needed in order to make its case were also confined to Moyamensing jail. They were kept in apartments that were supposed to be more comfortable than ordinary cells, and were paid $1.25 a day. Nevertheless, two of them disliked their surroundings sufficiently to want to escape. On November 9, two weeks before the trial began, they tied their blankets together, hooked them over the shutters of their unbarred windows, climbed down the rope of blankets, and successfully got away.

The citizens of Maryland, who followed closely all news of the Christiana arrests, believed that jail officials had helped those two witnesses escape. To them it was proof that there was no hope for a fair trial in abolitionist-tainted Pennsylvania if even the jailers were on the side of the blacks! The fact that the United States marshal, Anthony Roberts, who was in charge of the prisoners, was a good friend of Thaddeus Stevens confirmed their worst suspicions.

Marylanders were determined nevertheless to see that justice was done to the murderers of a prominent Maryland citizen. To make sure, they wanted to have some of their own men play a role in the prosecution. Just a week before the trial was to begin, the United States district attorney, John Ashmead, who was preparing his case against the so-called traitors, was notified by the district attorney for Maryland, Robert J. Brent, that he expected to play a prominent role in the trial, assisted by two other lawyers, James Cooper and Robert M. Lee, representing the Gorsuch family.

Ashmead was stunned. Two other lawyers, his cousin George Ashmead and James Ludlow, were already assisting him. Daniel Webster himself was urging that they prepare as strong a case as possible, and the three had been hard at work, planning their presentation and gathering more witnesses. An additional three lawyers joining the prosecution on behalf of Maryland would only cause trouble and confusion. The three would have their own ideas of how to develop a strategy. And courtesy would require that they be allowed to make major presentations to the court—which might run counter to the very arguments that Ashmead and his group were prepared to make.

At first, therefore, Ashmead politely declined the Maryland offer, saying he already had sufficient legal help to prosecute the case. Whereupon the governor of Maryland turned around and complained to the White House, and the White House instructed Ashmead to make some accommodation to the southerners.

Ashmead next offered the role of leading attorney in the case to Marylander Robert Brent, who declined, and then to James Cooper, who accepted. The prosecution now had six lawyers instead of three, which only resulted in a weaker rather than a stronger presentation. In some cases the men actually contradicted each other's line of reasoning. The defense took gleeful advantage of the confusion.

The trial was to be held on the second floor of Old Independence Hall in Philadelphia. The room was redecorated in honor of the occasion. Gas fixtures were installed in case night sessions were necessary, and ventilators put in the ceiling to keep the air from becoming stuffy.

The trial opened on Monday, November 24, to a packed courtroom. The handsome and historic hall was far too small to house all the people who wanted to attend, so many were turned away. The Marylanders denied admission again thought they were being discriminated against. One prominent citizen who had been refused later complained that while he was turned away, the hall was filled with Quaker ladies and blacks from Philadelphia.

Many journalists lined up each morning to find seats. Newspapers all over the United States had proclaimed the trial a test to determine if the Fugitive Slave Law could be enforced and the Compromise of 1850 upheld. Reporters came from far and near to provide their own locality with a firsthand account. Even overseas, people kept abreast of the famous treason trial.

Some of the excitement is described in a letter an Episcopal clergyman wrote to a friend in Washington:

> I have just visited [two of] the prisoners in the great Lancaster treason case (which is filling the papers at present) who are confined to Moyamensing jail which you know is in the vicinity of our house. They are respectable Quakers named Scarlett and Lewis. They showed me a book containing the names of about 600 persons who have visited them since their incarceration. By the way, this Christiana Slave Case is setting our citizens completely beside themselves. Court room crowded to overflowing, eloquent speeches, etc. One of the defendant's counsel, Theodore Cuyler, Esq, who is acquitting himself very creditably was a college friend of mine.

In addition to Cuyler, the counsel for the defense included James M. Read, Thaddeus Stevens, and W. Arthur Jackson. On the bench were the Honorable John Kane and Robert C. Grier.

Hanway was to be tried first alone, for treason. If

he was convicted, then the others would be tried separately for treason. If he was found innocent of that charge, then he and the others would face lesser charges.

Considering all the anticipation, the first three days of the trial were rather dull. Hanway was formally accused of the crimes attributed to him by the grand jury and pleaded not guilty. The rest of the time was spent in selecting a jury of twelve from 108 men called from all over Pennsylvania. Many of those called did not want to serve on a jury, but the two judges were very strict about letting prospective jurors off jury duty. They refused to release two bank presidents, both of whom claimed they were indispensable at their work, and they cross-examined all who claimed they were ill. So many of the prospective jurors tried to get off duty by claiming that they were deaf that Judge Grier remarked that "it seems the whole country is becoming deaf—an epidemic, I am afraid is prevailing."

The remaining jurors were then interviewed by both the defense and the prosecution, and twelve men were finally selected by Wednesday afternoon, November 26. Only eleven of these were sworn in. The twelfth was deliberately delayed until Friday, November 28, so that the jury was not closeted, and the jurors were allowed to go home for Thanksgiving, which was November 27.

The Marylanders pressing charges decided not to make the journey home for a single day, and spent most of Thanksgiving Day with their lawyers. An entry in Dickinson Gorsuch's journal makes it sound like a dreary time: "Thursday, November 27. Thanksgiving

Day. This has been a great holiday here; there was no court today. We went to Mr. Ashmead's office and stayed a while. John Bacon went home after the clothes I wore when I was shot."

At Moyamensing prison, however, there was a full-scale turkey dinner for the defendants. The abolitionist newspaper, the *Pennsylvania Freeman,* described the occasion:

> It affords us great pleasure to state that the Christiana prisoners were not wholly forgotten on Thursday last in the distribution of the good things pertaining to Thanksgiving. Thomas Kane, Esq. (son of the judge) sent to the prison for their use six superior turkeys, two of them extra size together with a pound cake, weighing 15 pounds. The turkeys were cooked with appropriate fixings, by order of a Mr. Freed, the Superintendent, in the prison kitchen, by a female prisoner detached for the purpose. The dinner for the white prisoners, Messrs Hanway, Lewis, and Scarlett, was served in appropriate style in the room by Mr. Morrison, one of the keepers. The U. S. Marshal. A. E. Roberts, Esq. several of the keepers, and Mr. Haws, one of the prison officers, dined with the prisoners as their guests. Mayor Gilpin coming, accepted an invitation to test the quality of the pound cake. Mrs. Martha Hanway, who has the honor of being the wife of the "traitor" of that name, and who has spent most of her time with her husband since his incarceration, served each of the

27 colored traitors with a plate of turkey, potatoes, pound cake, and the supply not being exhausted, all the prisoners on the same corridor were similarly supplied.

(When they read this item in the newspaper, the Maryland lawyers were so angry that one of them attempted to read it into the record in the courtroom. The judges, however, ruled it out of order.)

The case was resumed on Friday, November 28. District Attorney John M. Ashmead opened for the prosecution with a speech that lasted for an hour and a half. He explained to the jury that treason was defined in the Constitution as levying war against the United States and as uniting with its enemies by giving them aid and comfort. He then cited legal precedents for the opinion that the assemblage of a group of men for the purpose of making war was itself an act of war. If a group of men assembled with the intention of preventing by force the execution of one of the general laws of the United States, this too was such an act of war, he claimed.

To prove that Castner Hanway was indeed a traitor, he charged him with the following overt acts: 1) Assembling with others to make war against the United States; 2) resisting and opposing Kline; 3) rescuing the escaped slaves; 4) conspiring beforehand to resist the law; and 5) preparing and distributing literature urging people to resist the Fugitive Slave Act.

Ashmead also argued that before Hanway's appearance at the scene of the riot, the blacks had been discouraged, that Kline had ordered his party to leave before they were fired upon, and that Gorsuch had no weapon.

> Had he [Hanway] chosen to discountenance this flagrant violation of the law, and held the excited and infuriated blacks in check, the reputation of Pennsylvania would never have been tarnished by the disgraceful occurrences at Christiana, and a worthy and respected citizen of an adjoining state would not have been wantonly and wickedly murdered in cold blood, while engaged in the assertion of his legal rights. On Castner Hanway, especially rests the guilt of the innocent blood which was spilt on that occasion.

To make his case Ashmead would have to prove that Hanway had been part of an organized effort to resist the Fugitive Slave Law, that he had come to Parker's by prearrangement, and that he led rather than restrained the blacks, even ordering them to fire.

After other minor legal matters were attended to, Henry Kline was brought to the witness stand and kept there the rest of Friday and all day Saturday. He gave his side of the story, insisting that the blacks cheered at Hanway's arrival, that both Lewis and Hanway refused to obey his direct order to assist him, and that Hanway urged the blacks to begin firing. He claimed that after Hanway spoke with him, the miller rode his horse among the blacks milling about in the lane, and said something in a low voice to them. Immediately one of the blacks shouted "he's only a deputy" and after this the firing began.

Kline also stated that he did not run away, but only went twenty or thirty yards into the cornfield and then returned to assist the wounded Dickinson. This became a point that was argued back and forth for the rest of the trial.

As a witness Kline left a good deal to be desired. He was quite deaf, had a high piercing voice, spoke fast, and often did not hear the questions asked him. At the time of the riot he had had a bristling dark beard that was now gone. Some people wondered if he were trying to make himself look less villainous.

Kline spoke so glibly of this man and that man at the riot that the lawyers for the defense thought it was important that the marshal be asked to identify the prisoners he had actually seen at Parker's house. They asked that all of them be brought into the courtroom Saturday morning, and the judge agreed.

The appearance of the black prisoners in the courtroom created a sensation. They had all been freshly bathed and barbered, and wore new identical suits. Around each man's neck was a red, white, and blue scarf.

That same morning several newspaper reporters also noted the good-looking and tiny Lucretia Mott and several other Quaker women in the courtroom. They were knitting away furiously and did not even look up when the prisoners came in. The new outfits were their handiwork.

Once again Brent was incensed. The new outfits

provided for the prisoners seemed intended to confuse Kline and were proof once more that Philadelphians were on the side of the defendants.

Court having been resumed, Henry Kline completed his testimony and was followed by the remaining members of the Gorsuch party: Thomas Pearce, Joshua Gorsuch, Dickinson Gorsuch, Nicholas Hutchings, and Nathan Nelson. Out of respect for the dead man, Castner Hanway asked his lawyers not to cross-examine the two Gorsuches, but both testified that they had not actually heard Kline order Hanway to do anything, and that Kline himself had fled before the firing took place.

On Monday the prosecution presented more witnesses, including Miller Knott and his son, Alderman Reigart from Lancaster, and Sheriff William Proudfoot from Christiana. The two Knotts simply described coming on the scene after the riot, and finding Edward Gorsuch dead and Dickinson seriously wounded. The law officers told of Kline's attack on Hanway and Lewis when they came to Zercher's Hotel to give themselves up.

Another witness, Charles Smith, related that Samuel Williams, the black from the vigilance committee, had come to his house evidently by mistake and had given him the message that the Gorsuch party was on its way, and asked him to inform the slaves. Though the prosecution pressed him, Smith insisted he was not asked to inform the abolitionists.

Dr. Augustus Cain was then called to the witness stand, and asked if he had attended any meetings, "having been held in that neighborhood in regard to the Act of Congress in regard to fugitive slaves." Cain said he had attended an antislavery meeting in Horticulture Hall in West Chester where that subject had probably been alluded to, but that he had not seen Hanway there, and he had been a mere spectator.

Three of the black prisoners were examined in rapid order. One testified that Joseph Scarlett rode up to his house at daybreak and said that there were kidnappers at Parker's and "to let the colored people know." Another told of Elijah Lewis coming up to him in the fields and saying that there were kidnappers at Parker's, and it was "no time to take up potatoes now."

Dickinson Gorsuch was called back to the stand and asked to show the coat in which his father had been shot. Then to the utter surprise of everyone, the prosecution rested its case.

Considering the charges that Ashmead had made three days before, practically nothing had been proved against Hanway. There was no evidence to link him to any abolitionist activity, let alone prior knowledge of the coming of the Gorsuch party. There was no proof that he had done anything on the morning of September 11 but go to Parker's at the request of Elijah Lewis to see what was happening. If he refused to assist the marshal, there was no one's word but Kline's for this.

The *Pennsylvania Freeman* commented:

We can only say that in our judgement, (and such, we believe is the almost if not quite universal opinion of those who have watched the progress of the trial) the Counsel for the Government have not only failed to substantiate their charge of treason, even under their own absurd definition of that offense, but to show that the prisoner was guilty of any other violation of the law than that involved in a refusal to aid Kline and his party in arresting the fugitives. There was some pretty hard swearing on the part of the government witnesses, but the evidence in behalf of the defense will bring out enough of the truth to secure a prompt acquittal. We do not believe that any intelligent person anticipates the possibility of any other verdict than "not guilty."

CHAPTER 15

·•·

The Treason Trial Continued

O N TUESDAY, DECEMBER 2, THEODORE CUYLER OPENED for the defense. He began by attacking the presence of the Maryland lawyers.

The State of Maryland is here today, in the person of her Attorney General, and his coadjutors, a private prosecutor in a criminal case. Far be it from me to say, that she thirsts for the blood of this man; and yet I have seen events occur upon the trial of this case, which might almost justify that remark . . . Maryland distrusts the justice of Pennsylvania, and distrusts the faithfulness to their sworn duty of the officers of the General Government. She is here today by her own counsel, in what she regards as her own case.

Having pointed up the irregularities of the prosecution, he defended the Pennsylvanians as law-abiding, and said Hanway was a man of unblemished character who had only tried to do his civic duty. Cuyler also told about the earlier kidnappings that had so enflamed the valley. He described the events at Parker's, including Kline's flight, and spoke of Hanway's efforts to protect Pearce from the mob. Finally, he ridiculed the whole charge: "Sir, did you hear it? That three harmless, non-resisting Quakers, and eight and thirty wretched, miserable, penniless negroes, armed with corn cutters, clubs, and a few muskets, and headed by a miller, in a felt hat, without a coat, without arms, and mounted on a sorrel nag, levied war against the United States. Blessed be God that our union has survived the shock."

(Though colorful, Cuyler's description was not exactly accurate. Hanway, one of the three, was not a Quaker—though he looked like one—and only thirty-six blacks had been charged.)

The first witness for the defense was Thomas Penington, father-in-law of Marsh Chamberlain. Penington told of being at his daughter's house when the six men marched in uninvited and seized John Williams, and of watching the bloody battle that ensued through an air register from the floor above. He insisted that the men had not shown any warrant or identified themselves in any way.

The prosecution objected that this testimony was irrelevant, but the judges ruled it was just as proper for the defense to describe the state of feelings that existed in the valley because of the kidnappings as it was for the prosecution to attempt to prove that the neighborhood was prejudiced against the enforcement of the

Fugitive Slave Law.

Following Penington came a neighbor, then Mrs. Chamberlain, then her brother. All testified that they had recognized members of the Gap gang among the men who seized John. None knew, or were even told, whether John was in fact an escaped slave or a free man.

The prisoner Elijah Lewis next took the stand, in spite of objections from the government lawyers who thought he was a prejudiced witness, and gave a straightforward account of the riot. He insisted that Kline fled up the Long Lane to the Noble Road and did not return to the Parkers' until long after the battle, thus Kline was already far from the scene when the firing began, and that neither he nor Hanway had actually read the warrants. Neither had his glasses with him.

Lewis was followed by a series of minor witnesses. One of them related a conversation he had had with Dr. Thomas Pearce the night of the riot.

> He spoke to me of Hanway's defending him against the blacks. He did not detail the manner of that defense, but said he believed he owed his life to Hanway, those were his words in the matter as near as I can remember.
> Question: "Anything said about Kline?"
> Answer: "Yes, he commenced talking about Kline first, he spoke to me of Kline, before the attack was made, having been boasting all the time of his former feats of valor and induced them to believe he

was a man of great courage, but when they got on the ground, as soon as there was any evidence of danger, that his courage seemed to forsake him, and he left the ground."

Following this, the defense produced a number of witnesses who had known Kline a long time. Asked if his character was "good or bad," they all said it was "bad," or "very bad." A number answered in response to questioning that they would not necessarily believe anything Kline said under oath.

On Wednesday, December 3, there was a sensation in the courtroom when the defense brought to the stand John Carr, the employer of Harvey Scott. Scott was the young black who had testified at the preliminary hearings that he saw Henry Simms shoot Gorsuch. Now Carr announced to a hushed courtroom that on the night of the riot he had "buttoned" Scott up for the night into the loft where he slept and only "unbuttoned" him about daybreak the morning of the riot. Moreover, he could account for every move that Scott made until well after seven o'clock. Scott could not possibly have seen what he said he did.

If this was true, it demolished an important part of the case for the prosecution. Naturally, the prosecution cross-examined John Carr carefully. He explained that the ladder to Scott's loft passed through a room in which several of his granddaughters slept, and they preferred that Scott's door be locked after he had gone to bed for the night. Carr was asked if Scott could have escaped through the window in the course of the night.

He answered that it might have been possible, although Scott could never have gotten back into the loft without help.

Carr told the jury that a man had come to his blacksmith shop the afternoon of the riot and told both himself and Harvey Scott about the riot at Parker's. Hearing the details Scott had said, "I'm a nigger out of that scrape."

Another important witness Wednesday was Lewis Cooper (son-in-law of Elijah Lewis) who took Dickinson Gorsuch to the Pownalls' in his Dearborn wagon, and later took the body of Edward Gorsuch to Christiana. On that journey Dr. Thomas Pearce had ridden with him.

"He said it was one of the most imprudent acts his uncle [Edward Gorsuch] ever undertook, in fact, it was the most imprudent one he ever saw in his life," Lewis Cooper testified. "I do not recall the particulars, but he said more particularly, that Kline had left them, and that he called for his uncle to come away, and his uncle came out a marked distance, he took it to be ten yards, that far toward him, and he saw his uncle's countenance change suddenly, and he turned back and says 'my property is here, and I will have it or perish in the attempt.' "

Lewis Cooper then quoted directly from Thomas Pearce. " 'I thought it was very rash for my uncle to say so, and as soon as he had said this there came up a bright yellow negro, one of his own slaves, and shot him. I cannot say whether he shot him, but when he came up to my uncle with his hand extended, he fell dead. When I saw my uncle fall it was time to leave.' "

"To my understanding he (Dr. Pearce) got into the road somewhere, and saw Hanway, and runs to him and took hold of his saddle behind. Hanway keeping him between him and the negroes," Lewis Cooper concluded. "I understand him to hold by the saddle or skirt or something of that kind to assist in his flight."

Following Cooper, another neighbor came to the stand to describe the horn that was blown before dawn to call the laborers on the railroad to breakfast. Farmers too used horns to awaken their hands in the early morning. In this way it was established that the horn the Gorsuch party heard before their arrival was not necessarily a signal.

Finally, the defense produced a long string of witnesses to testify to the good character of Hanway. Since the miller had moved around a good deal, the witnesses came from various parts of the country. All spoke of him as quiet, law-abiding, and orderly. No one had ever known him to show the slightest interest in the abolitionist cause.

With these witnesses the defense closed its testimony on Thursday, December 4.

It was now the prosecution's turn for rebuttal, an attempt to disprove the testimony given on behalf of the defendants. The government lawyers first called a great many witnesses who said that Kline's character was "good." He had been a conscientious police officer in Philadelphia and he had made some enemies, but that was natural.

Next, to prove that there had actually been a conspiracy in the valley to resist the Fugitive Slave Law, the prosecution lawyers spoke of the meeting at the Bart Township schoolhouse on October 11, 1850, and described the difficulties of another Maryland slave owner who came to recapture his slaves in April of 1851. They also offered to prove that John Williams, the man taken and beaten at Marsh Chamberlain's farm, was actually a fugitive slave. All this evidence was ruled out of order by the judges, however, since new testimony cannot be introduced into a rebuttal. The prosecution should have offered the evidence much earlier in the trial, but were evidently prevented from doing so by confusion in their own ranks.

After a few more minor witnesses, Ashmead called the controversial Harvey Scott to the stand. It was the purpose of the defense to prove that the alibi given by his employer, John Carr, was not true, and that he was a witness to the murder of Gorsuch. The courtroom listened tensely to the following interrogation:

Mr. George Ashmead: Were you there on the morning of the 11th of September last?

Answer: I was proved to be there, but I was not there.

Question: On the morning of the 11th of September last?

Answer: No, sir. Kline swore I was there, and at the time I was taken up, I told the man I was not there, and they took me to Christiana, and I was frightened, and I didn't know what to say, and I said what they told me.

Mr. George Ashmead: I had a conversation with this witness three or four days ago, and he said he was there.

Judge Grier: Yes, others have had a conversation later than you.

Mr. George Ashmead: Do you understand my question when I ask you whether, on the morning of the 11th of September last, at Parker's house, you were present and saw what occurred?

Answer: That was what I said.

Question: Did you state that to me two or three days ago?

Judge Grier: Do you say so now?

Answer: No sir.

Question: Have you had a conversation with any one, since you conversed with me?

Answer: No sir.

Angry, the attorneys for the prosecution said they thought Harvey Scott was lying and should be tried for perjury. The lawyers for the defense answered that he was slightly feebleminded and had been scared into giving self-incriminating evidence. Judge Grier intervened to say he thought they should "let the poor devil go." The next day Thaddeus Stevens asked the prosecution to retract the intimation that the witness had been bribed or frightened into changing his story. This was done in the courtroom. However, after the trial was over one of the Maryland lawyers still maintained that the witness had been tampered with.

Looking into the case, Arthur Jackson, one of the defense lawyers, discovered that the only persons to visit

Harvey Scott in his prison cell directly before his change of testimony were members of the black vigilance committee. These men evidently persuaded Harvey to tell the truth in the courtroom, promising him that no harm would come to him. He believed them and did as they suggested.

With Harvey's testimony demolished, the case against Castner Hanway was weakened further. Nevertheless, the prosecution continued presenting witnesses in rebuttal. Dr. Pearce argued that Hanway did not save his life on purpose. It merely happened that Hanway's body was between the blacks and Pearce, and to save his own life Hanway begged them not to shoot. Dickinson Gorsuch then testified that he had seen Noah Buley at the riot. With this anticlimax the prosecution rested its case.

Now came one of the most exciting parts of the trial, the summing up. In the 1850s, long before radio, television, and commercial spectator sports, a good courtroom fight was a form of public entertainment. In this case, with excitement running high already, the final arguments were awaited as eagerly as the outcome of a horse race. Men and women crowded into the courtroom, and people watched for each issue of the daily paper to provide them with a report of the goings on in Independence Hall.

First came a speech by James Ludlow, counsel for the prosecution. He reviewed the laws of treason and the evidence against Hanway, hinted that Scott had been bribed, and ended by denouncing the abolitionists.

They would bury into oblivion the splendid memories of the past, and execrate the men who formed the constitution and the laws as themselves infamous traitors to humanity. They would bring upon this country of ours civil war, disunion, and all that is horrible. They would by their conduct destroy the lustre of humanity. They would tear from amid the firmament of nations the sun which has illumined them all. Talk to me of treason, of a few negroes headed by the prisoner at the bar! He was but acting upon principles which had been dictated to him by men in high authority, and who should have known better, from their knowledge of the laws and the constitution.

Joseph Lewis gave the principal speech for the defense. He began by saying that he thought the whole trial had been started in a moment of "public frenzy," and that if a little time had been taken to find out more about Castner Hanway, it would never have begun as a trial for treason.

It was pressure from Maryland that had made the trial necessary, Lewis suggested. Pennsylvanians deserved better treatment from their neighbors, since they had always been loyal and law-abiding in regard to the fugitive slave laws.

Pennsylvania puts no obstruction in the way of reclaiming fugitives, but only her own free citizens should not be unlawfully carried off. Was not this the position of Castner Hanway? Did he not act only as a Pennsylvanian should act? The whole evidence showed that he had only endeavored to see that no kidnapping was going on.

Our law merely says that no man can be carried into slavery, if a free man; if a slave, that no obstruction be placed in their way. This was the position of the prisoner. Is there a single thing he did not in according with his Pennsylvania feeling and Pennsylvania rights? There is no man that regrets this catastrophe more than Castner Hanway; that a citizen of Maryland should have been shot down, is regretted by him as by all others. This is shown by his direction to counsel that no questions should be asked of the two members of the Gorsuch family, who appeared to give evidence in this case.

The charge of treason—the continent from ocean to ocean is 3000 miles wide, and from the St. Lawrence to the Rio Grande, no less than 2000, and the extent of territory in this county is but a few acres wide; the occurrence was in the township of Sadsbury, between a cornfield and an orchard. Was this not an excellent place to raise an army? And this occurrence in the township of Sadsbury is treason? This was to overturn the General Government? Why, the accusation is so ridiculously absurd, that all is needed is to hold the matter up to view.

We are not trying the Fugitive Slave Law. The Fugitive Slave Law is trying itself. We apprehend that the South will be the first to be dissatisfied. That every man carried back to slavery will be an apostle of liberty, and the South will ask as boon that which she would now resist.

Robert Brent, the Maryland district attorney, next took the floor. He once more argued that it was correct for him to be present so that the citizens of Maryland might believe it was a fair trial. He then launched into an attack on the idea that a man had the right to disobey the law because he was conscientiously opposed to it. In this case the government would need a standing army to enforce any of its laws. It was a damnable, treasonable doctrine.

As for the fact that Hanway came to the riot without arms, Brent argued that it made no difference. "The Colored people then and there armed were his instruments of war; they were his arms, and I should have thought far more of Castner Hanway and Elijah Lewis if, while sympathizing with these blacks, if while determined to nullify and resist this law of Congress, they put on their armour, and led their soldiers in the fight. They would have been heroes in their way, and they would have resisted the law plainly, boldly, and openly."

If no witness had been found to demonstrate that Hanway was implicated in the conspiracy before the riot, this was because the whole neighborhood was traitorous, according to the Maryland attorney.

Brent's argument continued until Monday, December 8. He was followed by the equally long-winded John Read for the defense, who spoke for three days. Read discussed the constitutional issues in the case, questioned the Fugitive Slave Law, and criticized the case the prosecution had made. For instance, Kline, who was deaf, was supposed to have heard Hanway whisper to the blacks to shoot, although Kline himself was off in the woods long before the shooting began.

If the neighborhood was prepared to resist the Gorsuch party, it was Kline's own fault, Read pointed out. "He prowled up and down a peaceful country, drinking and carousing, and blustering about horse thieves, until all the slaves had notice of his coming. Had the Chief Marshal of this court been sent, instead of this prating villain, all the slaves within reach might have been arrested without loss of blood."

Everyone expected the great orator Thaddeus Stevens to speak next. Stevens, however, seemed to feel that the case against Hanway was so weak that his speech was unnecessary. To the great disappointment of the audience he declined.

The final speech for the prosecution was made by James Cooper. Cooper again summarized the evidence against Hanway, and called for his conviction.

It was now all but over. On December 11, 1851, just three months after the Christiana riot, Judge Robert Grier charged the jury, explaining once more and with care the laws of treason, and stating that it was his opinion that the act of defiance of the law was not widespread enough, nor was there enough evidence of a conspiracy to make the charge of treason stick.

Grier's charge to the jury was a thoughtful one, but he could not resist adding his own personal attack against the abolitionists:

With the exception of a few individuals, of perverted intellect, some small districts or neighborhoods whose moral atmosphere has been tainted and poisoned by male and female vagrant lecturers and conventions, no party in politics, no sect in religion, nor any respectable number of characters can be found within our border who have viewed with approbation or looked with any other feeling than abhorrence upon this disgraceful tragedy.

It is not in this Hall of Independence, that meetings of infuriated fanatics and unprincipled demagogues have been held to counsel a bloody resistance to the laws of the land. It is not in this city that conventions are held denouncing the Constitution, the laws and the bible. It is not here that the pulpit has been desecrated by seditious exhortations, teaching that theft is meritorious, murder excusable, and treason a virtue.

The guilt of this foul murder rests not alone on the deluded individuals who were its immediate perpetrators, but the blood stains with an even deeper dye the skirts of those who promulgated doctrines subversive of all morality and all government.

The jury, so charged, retired to their chambers in the American House, and returned to the courtroom fifteen minutes later. The clerk called their names and all answered present.

"Gentlemen of the Jury, have you agreed upon your verdict?" the clerk asked.

"Yes, sir," was the reply.

"Prisoner, stand up," the clerk then ordered. "Jurors look upon the prisoner. Prisoner look upon the jurors. How say you, Jurors, is Castner Hanway guilty of the Treason of which heretofore he stands indicted in the manner or form as he stands indicted, or not guilty?"

"Not guilty," the jurors chorused.

A ripple of sighs and smiles passed over the courtroom. Judge Grier had ordered the audience sternly not to express its opinion, but there was little doubt that the verdict was pleasing to those present.

Hanway, Lewis, and the others were now taken to the Lancaster prison to face the other charges still standing against them. In January they were again found not guilty. Kline was prosecuted for perjury at about the same time, but there was insufficient evidence to convict him. Samuel Williams, the informant of the vigilance committee, was given a separate trial for planning to defy the law, but also was found not guilty.

Though free, the defendants in the treason trial were left with heavy debts. They had had to pay all the expenses of their witnesses as well as of their lawyers. Since they had been found innocent, they petitioned the court to pay these debts, as had been done in the case of Aaron Burr. Judge Grier refused, however.

Instead, the black vigilance committees in New York City and Rochester as well as Philadelphia raised money for the black defendants, and Sadsbury Monthly Meeting of the Religious Society of Friends, through its Committee of Sufferings, paid the debts of Scarlett, Lewis, and Hanway, even though the latter was not a member. Deeply touched by this generous gesture,

Castner Hanway in 1853 joined the Progressive Friends of Longwood. This was an association of abolitionist Quakers who welcomed some non-Quakers to their ranks.

After its months on the front page of every newspaper, Christiana settled back thankfully to peaceful obscurity. There is no record of further kidnappings or rescues or other excitement until the Civil War. But that was perhaps because it had lost its dynamic black leader. William Parker had fled to Canada.

CHAPTER 16

PARKER'S ACCOUNT

His Trip to Canada

AFTER THE FIGHT, MY WIFE WAS OBLIGED, TO SE-crete herself, leaving the children in care of her mother, and to the charities of our neighbors. I was questioned by my friends as to what I should do, as they were looking for officers to arrest me. I determined not to be taken alive, and told them so; but, thinking advice as to our future course necessary, went to see some old friends and consult about it. Their advice was to leave, as, were we captured and imprisoned, they could not foresee the result. Acting upon this hint, we set out for home, when we met some female friends, who told us that forty or fifty armed men were at my house, looking for me, and that we had better stay away from the place, if we did not want to be taken. Abraham Johnson and Pinckney hereupon halted, to agree upon the best course, while I turned around and went another way.

Before setting out on my long journey north-ward, I determined to have an interview with my family, if possible, and to that end changed my course. As we went along the road to where I found them, we met men in companies of three and four, who had been drawn together by the excitement. On one occasion, we met ten or twelve together. They all left the road, and climbed over the fences into fields to let us pass; and then, after we had passed, turned, and looked after us as far as they could see. Had we been carrying destruction to all human kind, they could not have acted more absurdly. We went to a friend's house and stayed for the rest of the day, and until nine o'clock that night, when we set out for Canada.

The great trial now was to leave my wife and family. Uncertain as to the result of the journey, I felt I would rather die than be separated from them. It had to be done, however; and we went forth with heavy hearts, outcasts for the sake of liberty. When we had walked as far as Christiana, we saw a large crowd, late as it was, to some of whom, at least, I must have been known, as we heard distinctly, "A'n't that Parker?"

"Yes," was answered, "that's Parker."

Kline was called for, and he, with some nine or ten more, followed after. We stopped, and then they stopped. One said to his comrades, "Go on—that's him." And another replied, "You go." So they contended for a time who should come to us. At last they went back. I was sorry to see them go back, for I wanted to meet Kline and end the day's transactions.

We went on unmolested to Penningtonville; and, in consequence of the excitement, thought best to continue on to Parkersburg. Nothing worth mention occurred for a time. We proceeded to Downingtown, and thence six miles beyond, to the house of a friend. We stopped with him on Saturday night, and on the evening of the 14th went fifteen miles farther. Here I learned from a preacher, directly from the city, that the excitement in Philadelphia was too great for us to risk our safety by going there. Another man present advised us to go to Norristown.

At Norristown we rested a day. The friends gave us ten dollars, and sent us in a vehicle to Quakertown. Our driver, being partly intoxicated, set us down at the wrong place, which obliged us to stay out all night. At eleven o'clock the next day we got to Quakertown. We had gone about six miles out of the way, and had to go directly across the country. We rested the 16th, and set out in the evening for Friendsville.

A friend piloted us some distance, and we travelled until we became very tired, when we went to bed under a haystack. On the 17th, we took breakfast at an inn. We passed a small village, and asked a man whom we met with a dearborn, what would be his charge to Windgap. "One dollar and fifty cents," was the ready answer. So in we got, and rode to that place.

As we wanted to make some inquiries when we struck the north and south road, I went into the post-office, and asked for a letter for John Thomas, which of course I did not get. The postmaster scrutinized us closely,—more so, indeed, than any one had done on the Blue Mountains,—but informed us that Friendsville was between forty and fifty miles away. After going about nine miles, we stopped in the evening of the 18th at an inn, got supper, were politely served, and had an excellent night's rest. On the next day we set out for Tannersville, hiring a conveyance for twenty-two miles of the way. We had no further difficulty on the entire road to Rochester,—more than five hundred miles by the route we travelled.

Some amusing incidents occurred, however, which it may be well to relate in this connection. The next morning, after stopping at the tavern, we took the cars and rode to Homerville, where, after waiting an hour, as our landlord of the night previous had directed us, we took stage. Being the first applicants for tickets, we secured inside seats, and, from the number of us, we took up all of the places inside; but, another traveller coming, I tendered mine, and rode with the driver. The passenger thanked me; but the driver, a churl, and the most prejudiced person I ever came in contact with, would never wait after a stop until I could get on, but would drive away, and leave me to swing, climb, or cling on to the stage as best I could. Our traveller, at last noticing his behavior, told him promptly not to be so fast, but let all passengers get on, which had the effect to restrain him a little.

At Big Eddy we took the cars. Directly opposite me sat a gentleman, who, on learning that I was for Rochester, said he was going there too, and afterwards proved an agreeable travelling-companion.

A newsboy came in with papers, some of which the passengers bought. Upon opening them, they read of the fight at Christiana.

"O, see here!" said my neighbor; "great excitement at Christiana; a—a statesman killed, and his son and nephew badly wounded."

After reading, the passengers began to exchange opinions on the case. Some said they would like to catch Parker, and get the thousand dollars reward offered by the State; but the man opposite to me said, "Parker must be a powerful man."

I thought to myself, "If you could tell what I can, you could judge about that."

Pinckney and Johnson became alarmed, and wanted to leave the cars at the next stopping-place; but I told them there was no danger. I then asked particularly about Christiana, where it was, on what railroad, and other questions, to all of which I received correct replies. One of the men became so much attached to me, that, when we would go to an eating-saloon, he would pay for both. At Jefferson we thought of leaving the cars, and taking the boat; but they told us to keep on the cars, and we would get to Rochester by nine o'clock the next night.

We left Jefferson about four o'clock in the

morning, and arrived at Rochester at nine the same morning. Just before reaching Rochester, when in conversation with my travelling friend, I ventured to ask what would be done with Parker, should he be taken.

"I do not know," he replied; "but the laws of Pennsylvania would not hang him,—they might imprison him. But it would be different, very different, should they get him into Maryland. The people in all the Slave States are so prejudiced against colored people, that they never give them justice. But I don't believe they will get Parker. I think he is in Canada by this time; at least, I hope so,—for I believe he did right, and, had I been in his place, I would have done as he did. Any good citizen will say the same. I believe Parker to be a brave man; and all you colored people should look at it as we white people look at our brave men, and do as we do. You see Parker was not fighting for a country, nor for praise. He was fighting for freedom: he only wanted liberty, as other men do. You colored people should protect him, and remember him as long as you live. We are coming near to our parting-place, and I do not know if we shall ever meet again. I shall be in Rochester some two or three days before I return home; and I would like to have your company back."

I told him it would be some time before we returned.

The cars then stopped, when he bade me good by. As strange as it may appear, he did not ask me my name; and I was afraid to inquire his, from fear he would.

On leaving the cars, after walking two or three squares, we overtook a colored man, who conducted us to the house of—a friend of mine. He welcomed me at once, as we were acquainted before, took me up stairs to wash and comb, and prepare, as he said, for company.

As I was combing, a lady came up and said, "Which of you is Mr. Parker?"

"I am," said I,—"what there is left of me."

She gave me her hand, and said, "And this is William Parker!"

She appeared to be so excited that she could not say what she wished to. We were told we would not get much rest, and we did not; for visitors were constantly coming. One gentleman was surprised that we got away from the cars, as spies were all about, and there were two thousand dollars reward for the party.

We left at eight o'clock that evening, in a carriage, for the boat, bound for Kingston in Canada. As we went on board, the bell was ringing. After walking about a little, a friend pointed out to me the officers on the "hunt" for us; and just as the boat pushed off from the wharf, some of our friends on shore called me by name. Our pursuers looked very much like fools, as they were. I told one of the gentlemen on shore to write to Kline that I was in Canada. Ten dollars were generously contributed by the Rochester friends for our expenses; and altogether their kindness was heart-felt, and was most gratefully appreciated by us.

Once on the boat, and fairly out at sea towards the land of liberty, my mind became calm, and my spirits very much depressed at thought of my wife and children. Before, I had little time to think much about them, my mind being on my journey. Now I became silent and abstracted. Although fond of company, no one was company for me now.

We landed at Kingston on the 21st of September, at six o'clock in the morning, and walked around for a long time, without meeting any one we had ever known. At last, however, I saw a colored man I knew in Maryland. He at first pretended to have no knowledge of me, but finally recognized me. I made known our distressed condition, when he said he was not going home then, but, if we would have breakfast, he would pay for it. How different the treatment received from this man—himself an exile for the sake of liberty, and in its full enjoyment on free soil—and the self-sacrificing spirit of our Rochester colored brother, who made haste to welcome us to his ample home,—the well-earned reward of his faithful labors!

On Monday evening, the 23rd, we started for Toronto, where we arrived safely the next day. Directly after landing, we heard that Governor Johnston, of Pennsylvania, had made a demand on the Governor of Canada for me, under the Extradition Treaty. Pinckney and Johnson advised me to go to the country, and remain where I should not be known; but I refused. I intended to see what they would do with me. Going at once to the Government House, I entered the first office I came to. The official requested me to be seated. The following is the substance of the conversation between us, as near as I can remember. I told him I had heard that Governor Johnston, of Pennsylvania, had requested his government to send me back. At this he came forward, held forth his hand, and said, "Is this William Parker?"

I took his hand, and assured him I was the man. When he started to come, I thought he was intending to seize me, and I prepared myself to knock him down. His genial, sympathetic manner it was that convinced me he meant well.

He made me sit down, and said,—"Yes, they want you back again. Will you go?"

"I will not be taken back alive," said I. "I ran away from my master to be free,—I have run from the United States to be free. I am now going to stop running."

"Are you a fugitive from labor?" he asked.

I told him I was.

"Why," he answered, "they say you are a fugitive from justice." He then asked me where my master lived.

I told him, "In Anne Arundel County, Maryland."

"Is there such a county in Maryland?" he asked.

"There is," I answered.

He took down a map, examined it, and said, "You are right."

I then told him the name of the farm, and my

master's name. Further questions bearing upon the country towns near, the nearest river, etc., followed, all of which I answered to his satisfaction.

"How does it happen," he then asked, "that you lived in Pennsylvania so long, and no person knew you were a fugitive from labor?"

"I do not get other people to keep my secrets, sir," I replied. "My brother and family only knew that I had been a slave."

He then assured me that I would not, in his opinion, have to go back. Many coming in at this time on business, I was told to call again at three o'clock, which I did. The person in the office, a clerk, told me to take no further trouble about it, until that day four weeks. "But you are as free a man as I am," said he. When I told the news to Pinckney and Johnson, they were greatly relieved in mind.

I ate breakfast with the greatest relish, got a letter written to a friend in Chester County for my wife, and set about arrangements to settle at or near Toronto.

We tried hard to get work, but the task was difficult. I think three weeks elapsed before we got work that could be called work. Sometimes we would secure a small job, worth two or three shillings, and sometimes a smaller one, worth not more than one shilling; and these not oftener than once or twice in a week. We became greatly discouraged; and, to add to my misery, I was constantly hearing some alarming report about my wife and children. Sometimes they had carried her back into slavery,—sometimes the children, and sometimes the entire party. Then there would come a contradiction. I was soon so completely worn down by my fears for them, that I thought my heart would break. To add to my disquietude, no answer came to my letters, although I went to the office regularly every day. At last I got a letter with the glad news that my wife and children were safe, and would be sent to Canada. I told the person reading for me to stop, and tell them to send her "right now,"—I could not wait to hear the rest of the letter.

Two months from the day I landed in Toronto, my wife arrived, but without the children. She had had a very bad time. Twice they had her in custody; and, a third time, her young master came after her, which obliged her to flee before day, so that the children had to remain behind for the time. I was so glad to see her that I forgot about the children.

The day my wife came, I had nothing but the clothes on my back, and was in debt for my board, without any work to depend upon. My situation was truly distressing. I took the resolution, and went to a store where I made known my circumstances to the proprietor, offering to work for him to pay for some necessaries. He readily consented, and I supplied myself with bedding, meal, and flour. As I had selected a place before, we went that evening about two miles into the country, and settled ourselves for the winter.

When in Kingston, I had heard of the Buxton settlement, and of the Revds. Dr. Willis and Mr. King, the agents. My informant, after stating all the particulars, induced me to think it was a desirable place; and having quite a little sum of money due to me in the States, I wrote for it, and waited until May. It not being sent, I called upon Dr. Willis, who treated me kindly. I proposed to settle in Elgin, if he would loan means for the first instalment. He said he would see about it, and I should call again. On my second visit, he agreed to assist me, and proposed that I should get another man to go on a lot with me.

Parker's Account

Abraham Johnson and I arranged to settle together, and, with Dr. Willis's letter to Mr. King on our behalf, I embarked with my family on a schooner for the West. After five days' sailing, we reached Windsor. Not having the means to take us to Chatham, I called upon Henry Bibb, and laid my case before him. He took us in, treated us with great politeness, and afterwards took me with him to Detroit, where, after an introduction to some friends, a purse of five dollars was made up. I divided the money among my companions, and started them for Chatham, but was obliged to stay at Windsor and Detroit two days longer . . .

Chatham was a thriving town at that time, and the genuine liberty enjoyed by its numerous colored residents pleased me greatly; but our destination was Buxton, and thither we went on the following day. We arrived there in the evening, and I called immediately upon Mr. King, and presented Dr. Willis's letter. He received me very politely, and said that, after I should feel rested, I could go out and select a lot. He also kindly offered to give me meal and pork for my family, until I could get work.

In due time, Johnson and I each chose a fifty-acre lot; for although when in Toronto we agreed with Dr. Willis to take one lot between us, when we saw the land we thought we could pay for two lots. I got the money in a little time, and paid the Doctor back. I built a house, and we moved into it that same fall, and in it I live yet.

When I first settled in Buxton, the white settlers in the vicinity were much opposed to colored people. Their prejudices were very strong; but the spread of intelligence and religion in the community has wrought a great change in them. Prejudice is fast being uprooted; indeed, they do not appear like the same people that they were. In a short time I hope the foul spirit will depart entirely.

I have now to bring my narrative to a close; and in so doing I would return thanks to Almighty God for the many mercies and favors he has bestowed upon me, and especially for delivering me out of the hands of slaveholders, and placing me in a land of liberty, where I can worship God under my own vine and fig-tree, with none to molest or make me afraid. I am also particularly thankful to my old friends and neighbors in Lancaster County, Pennsylvania—to the friends in Norristown,

Quakertown, Rochester, and Detroit, and to Dr. Willis of Toronto, for their disinterested benevolence and kindness to me and my family. When hunted, they sheltered me; when hungry and naked, they clothed and fed me; and when a stranger in a strange land, they aided and encouraged me. May the Lord in his great mercy remember and bless them, as they remembered and blessed me.

Parker's
Account

EPILOGUE

IN HIS STORY OF HIS ESCAPE PARKER DOES NOT MEN-
tion the names of the friends who sheltered him.
There was good reason for this. He first wrote the articles before the Civil War, when many conductors of the
underground railroad would have been in real trouble
if their role had come to light. Later, when he published the articles in the *Atlantic Monthly* in 1866,
feelings ran so high in many communities that it was
still unwise to use real names.

Old accounts of the underground railroad in Lancaster and Chester counties contain several accounts of
Parker's escape. These do not entirely agree with Parker's own story nor that of Frederick Douglass. Nevertheless, they are probably partly true, at least.

The friend with whom Parker stayed in Rochester
was the man he had greatly admired since 1843, the
ex-slave and famous orator, Frederick Douglass. In his
autobiography, *My Life and Times,* Douglass wrote
about the visit:

A decided check was given the execution of the law (the Fugitive Slave Law) at Christiana, Penn., where three colored men, being pursued by Mr. Gorsuch and his son, slew the father, wounded the son, and drove away the officers and made their escape to my home in Rochester. The work of getting these men safely into Canada was a delicate one. They were not only fugitives from slavery but charged with murder, and officers were in pursuit of them. There was no time for delay. I could not look upon them as murderers. To me, they were heroic defenders of the just rights of man against manstealers and murderers. So I fed them, and sheltered them in my house. Had they been pursued then and there, my home would have been stained with blood, for these men who had already tasted blood were well armed and prepared to sell their lives at any expense to the lives and limbs of their probable assailants. What they had already done at Christiana and the cool determination which showed very plainly especially in Parker (for that was the name of the leader) left no doubt on my mind that their courage was genuine and that their deeds would equal their words. The situation was critical and dangerous. The telegraph had that day announced their deeds at Christiana, their escape, and that the mountains of Pennsylvania were being searched for the murderers. These men had reached me simultaneously with this news in the New York papers. Immediately after the occurrence at Christiana they, instead of going into the mountains, were placed on a train which brought them to Rochester. They were thus almost in advance of the lightning, and much in advance of probable pursuit, unless the telegraph had raised agents already here. The hours they spent at my house were therefore hours of anxiety as well as of activity. I dispatched my friend Miss Julia Griffiths to the landing three miles away on the Genesee River to ascertain if a steamer would leave that night for any port in Canada, and remained at home myself to guard my tired, dust-covered, sleeping guests, for they had been harassed and traveling for two days and nights, and needed rest. Happily for us the suspense was not long, for it turned out that that very night a steamer was to leave for Toronto, Canada.

This fact, however did not end my anxiety. There was danger that between my house and the landing or at the landing itself we might meet trouble. Indeed, the landing was the place where trouble was likely to occur if at all. As patiently as I could, I waited for the shades of night to come on, and then put the men in my "Democrat carriage," and started for the landing on the Genesee. It was an exciting ride, and somewhat speedy withal. We reached the boat at least fifteen minutes before the time of its departure, and that without remark or molestation. But those fifteen minutes seemed much longer than usual. I remained on board until the order to haul in the gangplank was given; I shook hands with my friends, received from Parker the revolver that fell from the hand of Gorsuch when he died, presented now as a token of gratitude and a memento of the battle for Liberty at Christiana and I returned to my home with a sense of relief which I cannot stop here to describe. This affair at Christiana, and the Jerry rescue at Syracuse, inflicted fatal wounds on the fugitive slave bill. It became thereafter almost a dead letter, for the slaveholders found that not only did it fail to put them in possession of their slaves, but the attempt to enforce it brought odium upon them and weakened the slave system.

Once safely in Canada, Parker was met by the Reverend Hiram Wilson, the underground railroad at Saint Catharines, and helped on his way to Toronto. In April he and Abraham Johnson arrived in the Buxton settlement, near Chatham, Ontario, and there each bought a fifty-acre farm.

A black journalist, Henry Bibb, who published *The Voice of the Fugitive,* in nearby Sandwich welcomed him effusively:

This man in our estimation deserves the admiration of a Hannibal, a Toussaint L'Ouverture, or a George Washington. A nobler defense was never made in belief of human liberty upon the plains of Lexington, Concord or Bunker Hill than was put forth by William Parker at Christiana. We bid him and his family and all others from the hypocritical republic welcome to this glorious land of our adoption, where no slave hunter dare to set his foot in search of a slave.

The Buxton settlement had been founded in 1849 by a Presbyterian minister, Dr. William King, as a haven of freedom for fifteen slaves he had inherited from a Louisiana wife. Dr. King wanted not only to set his own slaves free and give them an optimum chance for a better life; he also wanted to prove that with the proper environment ex-slaves would quickly become useful and productive citizens.

At Buxton the settlers each bought a fifty-acre lot, paying for it at the rate of $12.50 a year for ten years. There were strict regulations about the size and aspect of the house to be built upon the land and the gardens around it. Otherwise the community was self-governing. King was eager that all his settlers attend both church and school, but he did not make it compulsory.

For a man like Parker, whose intelligence and leadership qualities had found little outlet under slavery, Buxton was a paradise. He quickly enrolled in the adult night school and learned to read and write in no time. Within a year he became the Buxton correspondent for the *North Star,* an abolitionist newspaper edited by Frederick Douglass in Rochester.

At first the white residents of Raleigh Township opposed the establishment of the Buxton community and fought the integration of the schools, but they soon observed the determination and industriousness of the Buxton settlers and gave them a warmer welcome. Parker was one of those who contributed to the easing of relationships. He was universally liked and elected year after year to the Raleigh Township Council by blacks and whites alike.

Although they were safe and comfortable in Canada, many of the fugitives still thought of the United States as home and looked forward to the day they could return. During the tumultuous 1850s they watched with concern the progress of public opinion in the United States in regard to slavery.

That progress was slow. Despite Frederick Douglass's optimistic words, the Fugitive Slave Law continued to be enforced. In Boston, in 1854, a slave named Anthony Burns was captured and returned to his master in spite of heroic efforts on the part of the local vigilance committee to free him. Such defeats plunged both blacks and white abolitionists into deep gloom. The Dred Scott decision of 1857 was an even worse setback. According to the Supreme Court decision of that year, a slave could not gain his freedom by living in a Northern state or a territory declared free by Congress. This would deprive masters of their property without due process of law, the Supreme Court said.

Parker and his friends watched the newspapers as "free soil" versus proslavery settlers struggled for control of Kansas, and were thrilled by John Brown's efforts to start a slave uprising at Harpers Ferry, Virginia, though saddened by his subsequent execution.

Even after Abraham Lincoln was elected President, and South Carolina led the secession of the southern states, even after the Civil War began, the blacks remained uneasy. Lincoln repeatedly stated that he was fighting to save the Union, not to abolish slavery, and continued in fact to support the Fugitive Slave Law. In areas under the control of Union troops, blacks who escaped were returned to their masters, and when several Union generals rashly proclaimed slaves under their jurisdiction to be free, Lincoln canceled the orders.

Then in January 1863, Lincoln delivered the Emancipation Proclamation. Although it did not free the slaves in the border states, but only in the rebel states, it indicated that liberty was becoming the government's war aim. Later that summer Lincoln won the respect of the Canadian blacks by sending an emissary to talk with them. He wanted, he said, their help in planning for the liberation of four million slaves in the United States.

At the same time the commander in chief relented and decided to allow the free blacks to fight as soldiers in the Civil War. Frederick Douglass and others had long been urging that blacks be given a chance to prove their courage and their patriotism by being enrolled as soldiers, but there had been bitter opposition from some of the white troops, and Lincoln had not dared listen to the plea.

Now suddenly all this was changed, and Douglass entered into a lively campaign to raise black troops. Many Buxton settlers volunteered and joined the First Michigan Colored Infantry, which fought eleven major battles in North Carolina, Florida, South Carolina, and Georgia.

William Parker was over forty in 1863, but there

is an unconfirmed story that he too volunteered and saw service in the Union cause. Peter Woods, a teen-ager at the time of the Christiana riots, was a Union soldier, and reported seeing Pinckney in uniform down south. Where Pinckney was, Parker generally was too.

If Parker and Pinckney remembered their old masters vividly enough to return to fight against slavery, the South also remembered them. When General Robert E. Lee led his troops into Pennsylvania he is said to have asked the location of the town of Christiana, because he wanted to burn it down. (This does not really sound very much like Lee; perhaps it was some of his soldiers.) At any rate he never reached Christiana. He was stopped at Gettysburg by the Union troops.

After the war many Buxton settlers went south to help the newly freed slaves learn to read and write, and to start farming their own land. Some stayed on as colonists themselves in the South from which they had once fled in great fear.

As soon as the war was over, friends of Parker's sent his story to the *Atlantic Monthly*. The editor who received it explained his reactions:

The manuscript of the following pages has been handed to me with the request that I revise it for publication, or weave into its fact a story which would show the fitness of the southern black for the exercise of the right of suffrage. It is written in a fair, legible hand; its words are correctly spelled; its facts clearly stated, and—in most instances—its sentences are properly constructed. Therefore, it needs no revision. On reading it over carefully, I also discover that it is in itself a stronger argument for the manhood of the negro than any which could be adduced by one not himself a freeman, for it is the argument of facts, and facts are the most powerful logic.

The publication of Parker's story in the *Atlantic Monthly* created a stir in Christiana. Nevertheless, only six years later, when Parker himself came back to the village in 1872 to appear at a political rally, the white population of the town made little of the return of its famous ex-citizen.

The black population, however, welcomed their hero warmly. They were sad to learn that Eliza had died, but happy when Parker took an interest in Mrs. Simms, widow of Henry Simms, the man once accused of having killed old Mr. Gorsuch. When Parker took her back to Canada with him as his wife, the whole community wished them well.

For many years after that the Christiana riot was forgotten. The Parker house, known now as the old riot house, stood deserted in the midst of its orchard of unkept and gnarled apple trees. Children thought it was haunted, and no one said much about what had happened there.

In 1911 the Lancaster County Historical Society organized a commemoration of the riot. A medal was presented to a descendant of Edward Gorsuch, and another to Peter Woods, the only surviving person who had taken part. A memorial shaft was erected across the place where Zercher's Hotel had once stood.

The shaft still stands today. On one side is the name of Castner Hanway with the inscription, "He suffered for Freedom," and on the other the name of Edward Gorsuch with the words, "He died for the law." On a third side are the dates of the riot and the trials, and on the fourth, the names of all thirty-eight defendants.

Somewhere well down on the list of defendants is the name of William Parker. Otherwise there is no mention of his role in the event. Christiana had not yet grasped the fact that it was Parker's act of rebellion that had made history in the Octoraro Valley. Even today few people in the valley seem to know much about their black hero.

Rebellion in its public sense is the waging of war against legitimate authority. Judge Grier was right when he told the jury in the treason trial that the defiance of Parker and his comrades was not of a general enough or public enough nature to warrant the term treason. But there is another private sense to rebellion. It can mean the rebellion of one man who refuses to accept injustice and false logic in his lifetime and who makes his stand where he must. William Parker could see neither logic nor justice in the bland assumption that black men ought to obey laws that gave them no protection nor had ever won their consent.

"The laws of this country do not protect us," he had told Sarah Pownall the night before the riot, "and we are not bound to obey them. You whites have a country and may obey its laws, but we have no country."

The framers of the Declaration of Independence had said the same thing earlier: "Governments are instituted among Men, deriving their just powers from the consent of the governed," and "That whenever any Form of Government becomes destructive of these ends, it is the Right of the People to alter or to abolish it . . ."

While men and women remained slaves, they were governed without their consent, by illegitimate authority. Parker led his comrades in an act of rebellion that hastened the end of slavery and began the long slow process of extending the protection of the law, and a voice in formulating that law, to all Americans, whatever their color. The struggle to build a nation in which all citizens receive equal justice under the law continues today.

BIBLIOGRAPHY

Titles which are starred are especially recommended for young adult readers.

Campbell, Stanley W. *The Slave Catchers.* Chapel Hill, North Carolina: University of North Carolina Press, 1970.

Douglass, Frederick. *My Life and Times.* Hartford, Connecticut: Park Publishing, 1882.

Ellis, Franklin, and Evans, Samuel. *History of Lancaster County, Pennsylvania.* Philadelphia, 1882.

Forbes, David. *A True Story of the Christiana Riot.* Quarryville, Pennsylvania, 1898.

*Gara, Larry. *Liberty Line.* Lexington, Kentucky: University of Kentucky Press, 1961.

Hensel, W. U. *The Christiana Riot and the Treason Trials of 1851.* Lancaster, Pennsylvania: New Era Printing Co., 1911.

Jackson, Arthur. *A History of the Trials of Castner Hanway and Others for Treason.* Uriah Hunt & Sons, 1852.

Lewis, Walter. *Genealogy of the Family of Henry Lewis.* Schenectady, New York, 1951.

*Litwack, Leon. *North of Slavery*. Chicago: University of Chicago Press, 1961.

Lord and Lord. *Historical Atlas of the United States*. New York: Henry Holt, 1944.

*McPherson, James. *The Negro's Civil War*. New York: Pantheon Books, 1965.

―――. *The Struggle for Equality*. Princeton, New Jersey: Princeton University Press, 1964.

*Meltzer, Milton. *Thaddeus Stevens and the Struggle for Negro Rights*. New York: Thomas Y. Crowell, 1965.

*Merrill, Walter. *Against Wind and Tide*. A Biography of William Lloyd Garrison. Cambridge, Massachusetts: Harvard University Press, 1963.

Pease, William and Jane. *Black Utopias*. State Historical Society of Wisconsin, 1963.

*Quarles, Benjamin. *Black Abolitionists*. New York: Oxford University Press, 1969.

Robbins, James J. *Report on the Trial of Castner Hanway for Treason*. Philadelphia, 1852.

Seibert, Wilbur. *The Underground Railroad from Slavery to Freedom*. New York, 1898.

Smedley, R. C. *The History of the Underground Railroad in Chester County*. Lancaster, Pennsylvania, 1883.

Still, William. *The Underground Railroad*. Philadelphia: Porter and Coates, 1872.

*Ullman, Victor. *Look to the North Star. The Life of William King*. Boston: Beacon Press, 1969.

PERIODICALS

Browin, Frances W. "But We Have No Country." *Quaker History,* Autumn, 1968.

Douglass, Hugh. "The Christiana Riot, September 1851."

Journal of the Historical Society, Octoraro Area, vol. 3, no. 11, May 1971.

Grau, Richard. "The Christiana Riot, A Reappraisal." *Journal of the Lancaster County Historical Society,* vol. 68, 1964.

Hensel, W. U. "Aftermath of the Christiana Riot." *Journal of the Lancaster County Historical Society,* vol. 161, 1912.

Nash, Roderick. "William Parker and the Christiana Riot." *Journal of Negro History,* XLVI.

Whitely, Paul. "Friends in Lancaster County." *Journal of the Lancaster County Historical Society,* vol. 51, 1947.

Whitson, Thomas. "The Hero of the Christiana Riot." *Journal of the Lancaster County Historical Society,* vol. 1., 1896.

NEWSPAPERS CONSULTED

West Chester: *Village Record, American Republic.*

Philadelphia: *The North American, United States Gazette, The Bulletin, The Sun, Washington Republic.*

New York: *Times, Independent.*

Abolitionist: *Liberator, National Anti-Slavery Standard, Pennsylvania Freeman.*

ORIGINAL MANUSCRIPTS

Minutes, Sadsbury monthly meeting of the Religious Society of Friends.

Letter, Edward Jones to Mrs. Catalina Langdon, December 5, 1851.

Unpublished Manuscript. "Some Recollections of a Long and Unsuccessful Life." George Steele, 1918. Used with permission of Mrs. Barnard Levi Pownall.

INDEX

Ludlow, James, 173
Lynch law, 56

M

Marsh, Perry, 7, 138
Mathews, Elias, 62
McKenzie Tavern, 51
Mine Ridge, 6
Monkton (Maryland), 61
Moore, Jeremiah, 11, 13
Moore, Joseph, 53
Moore, Samuel D., 53
Morgan, John, 147
Mott, Lucretia, 153
Mount Vernon (N.Y.), 121
Moyamensing (prison), 137, 152
My Life and Times (Douglass), 195

N

Nelson, Nathan, 67, 84, 107, 111
New York Independent (newspaper), 144
Nine Points, 55
North Star (newspaper), 16, 199

O

Octoraro River, 116
Octoraro Valley, 204

P

Padgett, William, 7, 66, 131
Parker, William, 3, 43, 69–70, 73, 104, 112–113, 119, 180
  description of, 14–15
  escape of, 28–31
  evaluation of, 198–199
  fight against extradition of, 188–189
  flight to Canada of, 181–194
  on Fugitive Slave Law, 48
  marriage of, 52–53
  reaction to freedom of, 35–36
  resistance to kidnappers by, 46–48, 54–56
  role of, at Christiana, 2
Pearce, Dr. Thomas, 65, 67, 78, 84–86, 107, 111, 167, 169, 173
Penington, Thomas, 166
Pennsylvania Freeman (publication), 158, 163
Pequea Valley, 7
Philadelphia, 11
Philadelphia Bulletin (newspaper), 142
Philadelphia Sun (newspaper), 141
Philadelphia Vigilance Committee, 12, 73, 153
Pinckney, Alexander, 71,

Tubman, Harriet, 12
Tully, Thomas, 67

U

Underground railroad, 117
  and the Fugitive Slave
    Law, 37–38
  history of, 8
  importance of Sadsbury
    to, 13–14
  origin of the term, 9–10
  role of, to slaves, 1–2
United States commis-
  sioners. *See* Com-
  missioners, United
  States
United States Constitution,
  8

V

Voice of the Fugitive, the,
  198

W

Walker, Isaac, 52–53
Wallace, Jarett, 61–62
Washington Republic,
  (publication), 143
Webster, Daniel, 132, 154
Whig party, 145
Whipper, Benjamin, 50
Whitson, George, 57
Whitson, Moses, 49–51
Whitson, Thomas, 135
Williams, Allen, 55–56
Williams, Henry, 55
Williams, John, 58, 73
Williams, Samuel, 68, 73,
  93, 95, 162, 179
Wilson, Hiram, 198
Wood, Peter, 135–136
"Woolly Heads," 145

Z

Zercher's Hotel, 118, 130,
  132, 137–138, 204